EYES TO THE HILLS

To be able really to see, it is not enough to open the eyes,
one must first open one's heart

GASTON REBUFFAT

EYES TO THE HILLS

THE MOUNTAIN LANDSCAPE OF BRITAIN

GORDON STAINFORTH

CONSTABLE
LONDON

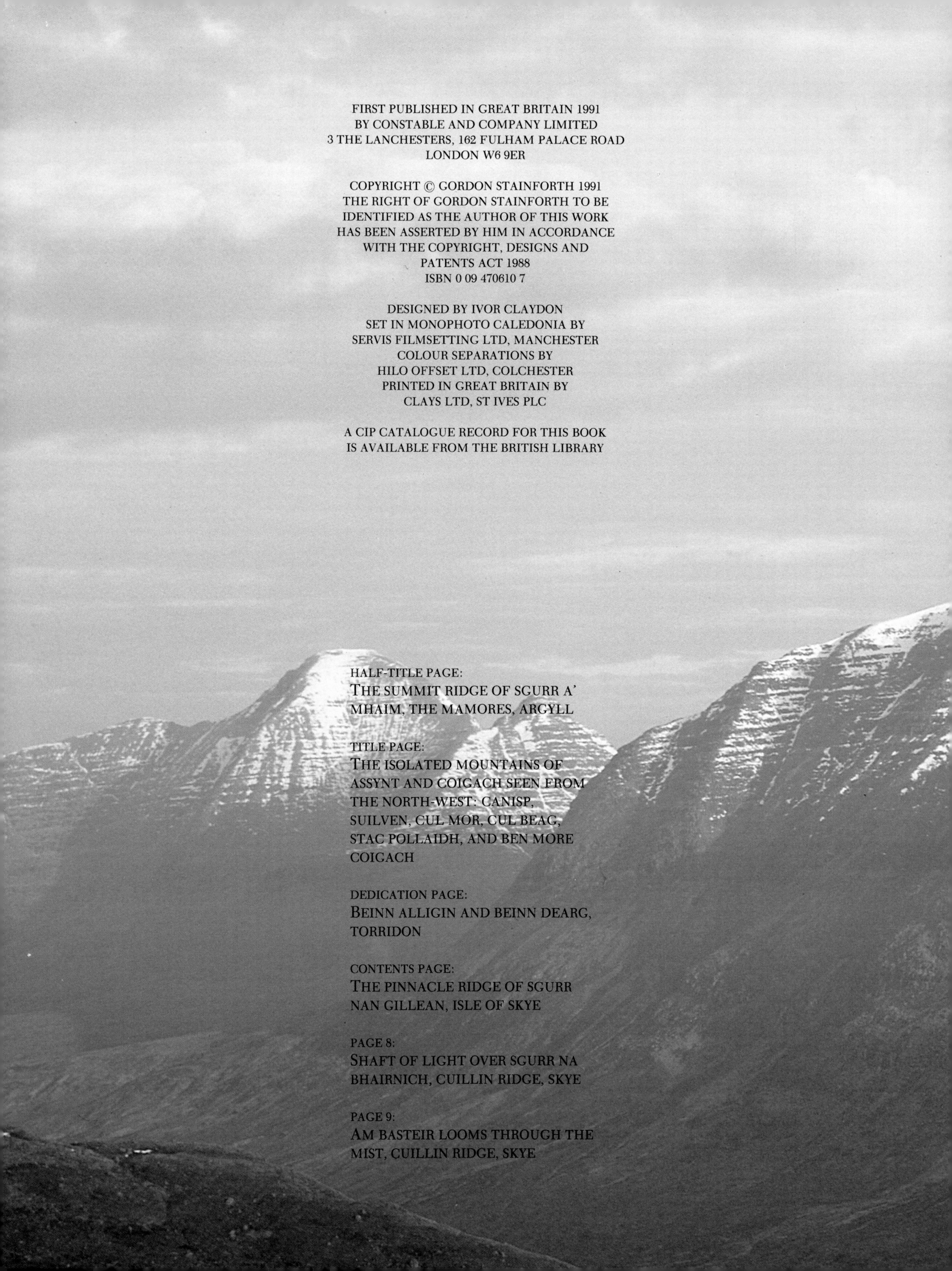

FIRST PUBLISHED IN GREAT BRITAIN 1991
BY CONSTABLE AND COMPANY LIMITED
3 THE LANCHESTERS, 162 FULHAM PALACE ROAD
LONDON W6 9ER

COPYRIGHT © GORDON STAINFORTH 1991
THE RIGHT OF GORDON STAINFORTH TO BE
IDENTIFIED AS THE AUTHOR OF THIS WORK
HAS BEEN ASSERTED BY HIM IN ACCORDANCE
WITH THE COPYRIGHT, DESIGNS AND
PATENTS ACT 1988
ISBN 0 09 470610 7

DESIGNED BY IVOR CLAYDON
SET IN MONOPHOTO CALEDONIA BY
SERVIS FILMSETTING LTD, MANCHESTER
COLOUR SEPARATIONS BY
HILO OFFSET LTD, COLCHESTER
PRINTED IN GREAT BRITAIN BY
CLAYS LTD, ST IVES PLC

A CIP CATALOGUE RECORD FOR THIS BOOK
IS AVAILABLE FROM THE BRITISH LIBRARY

HALF-TITLE PAGE:
THE SUMMIT RIDGE OF SGURR A'
MHAIM, THE MAMORES, ARGYLL

TITLE PAGE:
THE ISOLATED MOUNTAINS OF
ASSYNT AND COIGACH SEEN FROM
THE NORTH-WEST: CANISP,
SUILVEN, CUL MOR, CUL BEAG,
STAC POLLAIDH, AND BEN MORE
COIGACH

DEDICATION PAGE:
BEINN ALLIGIN AND BEINN DEARG,
TORRIDON

CONTENTS PAGE:
THE PINNACLE RIDGE OF SGURR
NAN GILLEAN, ISLE OF SKYE

PAGE 8:
SHAFT OF LIGHT OVER SGURR NA
BHAIRNICH, CUILLIN RIDGE, SKYE

PAGE 9:
AM BASTEIR LOOMS THROUGH THE
MIST, CUILLIN RIDGE, SKYE

IN MEMORY OF MY MOTHER
JUNE STAINFORTH (1920–1966)
WHO INSPIRED

CONTENTS

— 1 —
MOUNTAIN APPEARANCES

SAVAGE OR BEAUTIFUL?

'Beauty, horror and immensity-united' – that is how the landscape of the English Lake District was described by a typical tourist in the late eighteenth century.[1] So used are we today to superlative visual sensations that a tranquil scene like the LANGDALE PIKES FROM TARN HOWS (*opposite*) seems very tame to us, though certainly beautiful. What we have to realise is that before the eighteenth century it was very difficult for people to see any beauty in mountain scenery at all. It was regarded by the superstitious and the rational alike as wasteland, full of hidden dangers and entirely alien.

Yet before we scoff at this lack of appreciation we would do well to remember just how far the way we see is coloured by the values of the particular society in which we live. We can only ever perceive the world, in effect, through a dense filter of prejudice and fashion.

The similarity of several visitors' accounts of Loch Coruisk in the Cuillins in the early nineteenth century is particularly striking:

'I never saw a spot on which there was less appearance of vegetation of any kind; the eye rested on nothing but brown and naked crags. . . .'[2]

'Not a billow curled on the shore of the black lake, which like Acheron, seemed as if dead, and fixed in eternal silence. Not a bird was to be seen. . . .'[3]

'. . . no sound, nor sight of any moving thing – nothing but a dead and stony, seemingly, a God-forsaken world. We almost longed, in this cloud-capped thunder-stricken region, to hear the voice of a gladsome bird. . . .'[4]

It is as if each of these writers had simply read some of the existing accounts and rehashed them, or decided what they were going to see before they had even been there. And their preconceptions were so strong that, when they *did* get there, they were unable to remove the filters from their eyes. Or rather, they saw only what they *wanted* to see, and they didn't see what they didn't want to see.

The reader will perhaps be interested to see what LOCH CORUISK looked like through the unbiased eye of my camera on a

THE LANGDALE PIKES FROM TARN HOWS, CUMBRIA

fine summer's day in 1989 (*above*). It was a scene full of colour and the clamour of seagulls – and, quite incongruously, from the verdant island in the middle of the loch came the contented call of a solitary cuckoo.

This type of picture postcard view will serve as a very fair example of the way we prefer to see mountain landscapes today. They no longer threaten or frighten us, but are seen in a purely aesthetic, visual way, as an attractive backdrop of vaguely interesting peaks.

LOCH CORUISK, ISLE OF SKYE

RIGHT:
THE FIVE SISTERS OF KINTAIL

THE 'SUBLIME'

But there is a third, much more interesting way of seeing mountains – which the ancients had not found, and which we have largely lost – and that is as being both awesome and beautiful at the same time. Early mountain enthusiasts, like the 'typical tourist' I mentioned at the beginning, found that their sense of 'horror' did not prevent them from finding these tremendous objects rather attractive, in a strange way; the new-found pleasure of looking at mountains was, for them, much less to do with beauty than with excitement. They were not ashamed to admit that they found these awesome scenes thrilling.

Because this new type of beauty was not like beauty in the ordinary sense, these eighteenth-century travellers preferred to talk instead of the 'sublime'. Edmund Burke, who was the first to consider this new way of seeing in depth, defined the sublime by such paradoxical phrases as 'a sort of tranquility tinged with terror' and 'delightful horror'.[5] And because he regarded the element of shock or astonishment as 'the effect of the sublime in its highest degree', he concluded that the most important quality of all in a sublime landscape was 'vastness'; for only this, he said, has the unfailing ability to astonish us.[6]

However exaggerated this response to mountain scenery may seem to us today, we must admit that these early sightseers – who, it must be remembered, were unaccustomed to such landforms – were more likely than we are to be impressed by the wonders of nature. Nowadays we tend to reserve most of our enthusiasm for the achievements of man.

SGURR AN FHIDHLEIR, COIGACH

ILLUSORY AND EVERCHANGING

The archetypal first sighting of a 'sublime' mountain is a sudden, breathtaking glimpse of something impossibly high, awesomely big, and utterly otherworldly in appearance. So extraordinary is it that at first we are not quite sure what we are looking at. We cannot tell how big it is, and how steep different parts of it are. It is at the same time both very real and very unreal, a paradox of solid fact and dreamlike illusion. We are not quite sure, in a word, what the image is *made* of.

ICY LIATHACH LOOMS ABOVE GLEN TORRIDON

RIGHT:
BEINN ALLIGIN FROM THE EAST AT DAWN

18

STRANGE CLOUDS OVER SGURR
DUBH IN THE CUILLINS

LEFT:
LOOKING DOWN FROM BEN NEVIS
AT CLOUD POURING OVER MEALL
CUMHANN

PAGE 22:
AN TEALLACH FROM THE EAST AT
DAWN

PAGE 23:
THE SAME VIEW, A DAY LATER

And, if anything, the more we look at it, the more puzzling it
becomes. The brain attempts to supply hard facts, but the eye is
transfixed by the strange shifting effects of an optical illusion. The
apparition starts to 'slide about in our eyes', to use the climber J.
Menlove Edwards' memorable phrase.[7] And to complicate matters
still further, the vision really is changing even as we look at it. The
everchanging weather not only affects the way the scene is lit, but
physically – in the form of running water and accumulating snow –
it continually modifies the actual surface of the mountain. Because
a mountain can never be seen separately from the atmosphere of
the moment, the weather should be regarded as *part* of it; and it is
therefore literally never the same twice.

MOUNTAINS AS THEATRE

RIGHT:
SUILVEN AFTER FRESH SNOW

The appearance of a mountain is, then, extremely theatrical, full of illusion and visual trickery. In Britain's predominantly cyclonic climate, a summit will often be concealed for hours or even days at a time; and when the curtains part we are frequently presented with a major 'costume change' – new snow, for example, or a spate of streams that were not there before.

CLOUD CLEARING ON MULLACH AN RATHAIN, LIATHACH, AFTER A DAY OF SNOW

In addition, there is a whole range of other natural and rather magical 'special effects' that we may encounter, such as rainbows, lightning, snow plumes and 'Brocken spectres'. Not to mention some even less accountable phenomena, such as some mysterious circles I once came across on Brandon Mountain in County Kerry in south-west Ireland. . . .

A 'BROCKEN SPECTRE' SEEN FROM THE SUMMIT OF BEN NEVIS

PAGE 27:
CLOUD 'SMOKING' OFF SUILVEN AT DUSK

BELOW
MYSTERIOUS CIRCLES ON BRANDON MOUNTAIN, CO KERRY

BUILDING MOUNTAINS IN THE MIND

Because a mountain is so massive and difficult to travel around, and so often concealed by the weather, it is only ever revealed to us in glimpses. It is a series of transitory and ethereal 'appearances' rather than a single, solid object – an amalgam of different sightings rather than a permanent, unchanging thing.

No single viewpoint, of whatever height or angle – nor a large number of different viewpoints – will ever give us a true and complete picture of the whole mountain. Short of taking an extensive helicopter flight around it, we are left with the essentially creative task of piecing together a whole variety of disparate images – from different viewpoints, at different times, and in different weather conditions.

A mountain, as we observe and come to understand it, is a mental construct. To a much greater extent than we may be prepared to admit, it is 'moulded' by our imagination. More than we may realise, it is *our* landscape.

THE MIGHTY TRIPLE BUTTRESS OF
COIRE MHIC FHEARCHAIR EMERGES
FROM THE CLOUD AFTER A STORM

RIGHT:
SUILVEN FROM THE EAST AT DUSK

PAGE 28:
SUILVEN ON A STORMY EVENING

PAGE 29:
SUILVEN REFLECTED IN LOCH
MEALL A' MHUTHAICH AT SUNRISE

'SHADOWY PERSONALITIES'

THE NORTH FACE OF SGURR AN FHIDHLEIR

Because mountains have such a distinctive shape and presence, and yet are continually changing in appearance and mood, it is easy to start to regard them as 'shadowy personalities', as the Victorian mountaineer, Leslie Stephen, once called them.[8] In Britain this anthropomorphic tendency is reflected in many of our mountain names – from the Old Man of Coniston to the Old Man of Skye (the original name for the 'INACCESSIBLE PINNACLE' – *p.166*), with a host of young Maidens and Old Women in attendance, and all kinds of other strange characters like the COBBLER (*p.46*) and the FIDDLER (*above*). And, thanks to the unpredictable British weather, these old mountains of ours are as moody and temperamental as any in the world.

The danger of characterising mountains in this way is that we might start to talk about them, as poets and mystics sometimes do, as if they really were living beings. This way of speaking, which John Ruskin called 'the pathetic fallacy',[9] may have some legitimacy as a literary device if it describes how a scene affects our emotions in a strictly metaphorical way, but there is a risk that we will become so carried away by our metaphors that our true perception of the landscape will be hopelessly clouded.

An example of this fallacious way of thinking is the assertion made by the mystic, R.L.G. Irving, that by climbing TRYFAN (*below*) and Glyder Fach – 'getting to know them and loving to be with them' – he is giving them a personality. He actually goes so far as to claim that something of himself is in them and that, 'by the interchange of what we have given them and they have given us, there is a part of our personality in them and of theirs in us that is indestructible.'[10]

The idea that we can have a two-way communion with a lump of rock is, of course, utter nonsense. But this is the mistake of mysticism in general: it claims more than can meaningfully be said. Mountains do not feel anything, nor do they say anything. They just are.

TRYFAN FROM LLYN Y CASEG-FRAITH . . . IN FEBRUARY

These crags, and heaths, and clouds, how great they are, how lovely, how for ever to be beloved, only for their own silent, thoughtless sake!

JOHN RUSKIN (1856)

UPPER ESKDALE FROM BORDER END, CUMBRIA

THE LIVING ROCK

And yet, and yet. It seems that we can never quite rid ourselves of the idea that there is a definite spiritual presence in nature – that a piece of inanimate rock holds some inner secret. Stones of an unusual shape or colour still have a strange fascination for us, and often we cannot resist picking them up and taking them home with us.

One reason for this fascination is that, while there is a vast apparent gap between ourselves and the inanimate world, we know very well that in a basic sense there is no gap at all – that we are all made of the same dust and that we must all return to it. Dust to dust.

QUARTZ PEBBLE ON CAIRN GORM

RIGHT:
LICHEN ON A BOULDER IN COIRE ARDAIR, CENTRAL HIGHLANDS

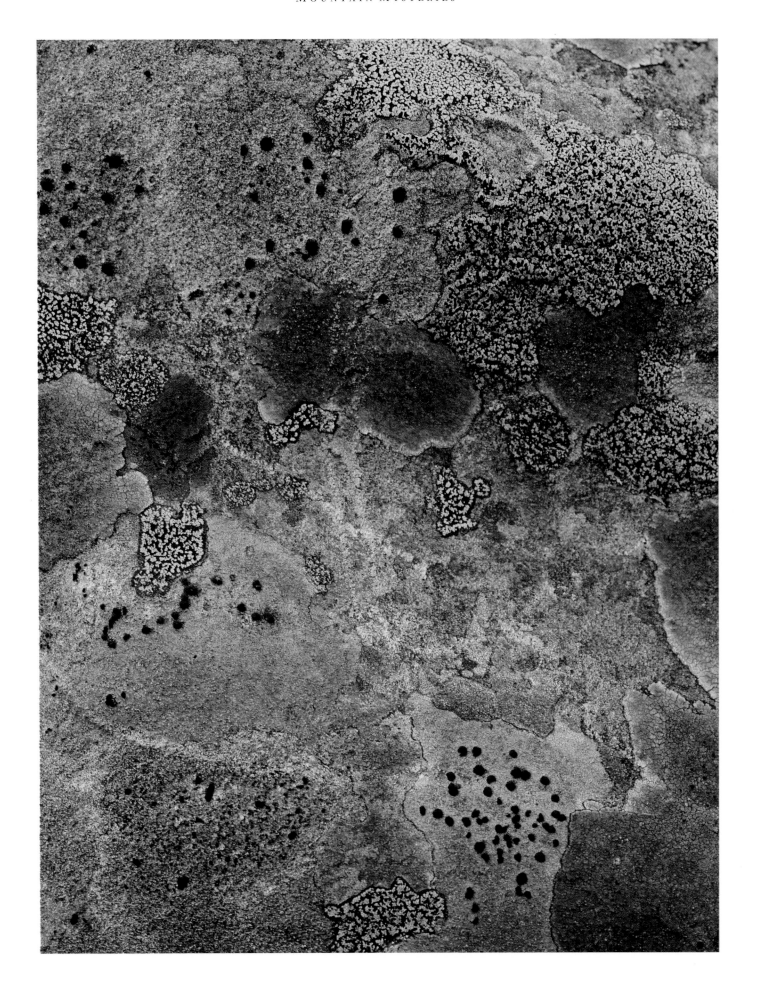

PEBBLES IN THE TORRENT OF ALLT
COIRE ARDAIR

LEFT:
GRANULITE BOULDER IN LOCHAN
A' CHOIRE ARDAIR

But it is the idea that rock is in some sense living that fascinates us most. For, with the development of subatomic physics, we now know that the mediaeval alchemists were indeed right when they said there is 'life in the stone'; and we are presented with the great new paradox that what appears so solid – rock-solid – and lifeless is actually a whirling mass of particles or 'energy packets', in a vast amount of space. We are told not only that there is energy in matter, but that matter is equivalent to energy. Rock remains a living mystery, its very substance a wonderful enigma – indeed the first great wonder of the world.

THE MYSTERY OF MATTER

LEFT:
FOLDED MICA-SCHIST BELOW THE
NORTH PEAK OF THE COBBLER

The thing that is most baffling and wonderful about matter is the most obvious – its hard substantiality; and no amount of science can either reduce or explain it. Our knowledge of subatomic particles cannot change the way we experience rock, or take away its basic mystery.

Yet while we are only too ready to wonder at the existence of mysterious particles, we seem reluctant today to marvel at the wonders of nature as we actually experience them. We are determined, it seems, not to treat the mysteries of the world as mysteries.

To acknowledge that matter itself is a mystery does not imply that there is a puzzle to be solved, or that we are somehow deprived. We have to come to see that the natural world as it is given to us is quite wonderful enough in itself. Nothing is lacking.

A LICHENOUS BOULDER ON SRON A'
CHOIT, LOCH MAREE, WESTER ROSS

MOUNTAINS AS SCULPTURE

THE GREAT CAULDRON OF COIRE
LAGAN SEEN FROM THE SUMMIT OF
SGURR ALASDAIR, SKYE

THREE-DIMENSIONAL ART

I have emphasised the mystery and wonder of matter itself because the fascination of a mountain's appearance cannot be separated from the enigma that lies behind it. Once we stop seeing a mountain simply as an astonishing, beautiful or awesome 'sight', we become interested in the thing itself – as a work of art. Our interest shifts from the two-dimensional and the pictorial, to the three-dimensional and the sculptural. Until we have some conception of the topography and substance of a mountain, our appreciation is limited to a strictly visual pattern of shapes and colours, a diverting arrangement of light and shade with a more or less distinctive or graphic outline.

We can apply just the same aesthetic criteria to mountains as to works of sculpture; and when we do so we will often be forced to admit that, as such, they are incomparably finer than anything

Mountain scenery is the antithesis not so much of the plains as of the commonplace. Its charm lies in its vigorous originality.

LESLIE STEPHEN (1894)

SUMMIT SCULPTURE ON BEN AVON,
THE CAIRNGORMS

THE EXTRAORDINARY SKYLINE OF
THE COBBLER

man can produce. With their extraordinary qualities of uniqueness
and unpredictability they have all the appearance of being the
work of a creative imagination. Everywhere are to be found the
sort of 'waving and serpentine lines' that William Hogarth
admired in nature, which lead the eye on a 'wanton kind of
chase'.[11] The uniqueness of line and form seems very much like
the product of an imagination run riot – experimenting at will – to
create something beautiful for its own sake.

CLOUD POURS OVER THE CUILLIN
RIDGE, ISLE OF SKYE

48

You cannot have, in the open air, angles, and wedges, and coils, and cliffs of cold. Yet the vapour stops suddenly, sharp and steep as a rock, or thrusts itself across the gates of heaven in likeness of a brazen bar; or falls into ripples like sand; or into waving shreds and tongues, as fire. On what anvils and wheels is the vapour pointed, twisted, hammered, whirled, as the potter's clay?

JOHN RUSKIN (1860)

It is difficult, when looking at such extravagant inventiveness, to avoid the question: why is so much of nature so unnecessarily beautiful? Why does so much of it look almost as if it were *designed* . . . to please the eye, and for no other reason? The landscape need not be nearly this interesting. We can easily imagine the British Isles without such beautiful freaks as AN TEALLACH (*opposite*), or Suilven, or the Cuillin Ridge, just as we can imagine a world without flowers – or a world with no mountains at all. Take away An Teallach or the Cobbler and we would not be any the wiser. They are an entirely unnecessary bonus, a gift from the gods.

AN TEALLACH, WESTER ROSS, AT
SUNRISE

LEFT:
THE BASTEIR TOOTH ON THE
CUILLIN RIDGE GLOWS IN THE
EVENING SUN

Unfortunately, many people are reluctant to see mountains in this way – as works of art – precisely because they are natural and not man-made. A Londoner to whom I recently showed the picture of the BASTEIR TOOTH (*opposite*), for example, admitted that if it were a giant man-made sculpture in Hyde Park he would indeed be impressed by it, but as a natural pinnacle on a remote mountain-top it left him quite cold.

The main reason for his attitude, I believe, was that he had never seen a mountain feature like this in the raw. Which only goes to support my argument that a mountain is something to be experienced in the round: it is not a piece of two-dimensional scenery – like a stage 'flat' or a backdrop – but a topographical intrusion that encroaches upon our three-dimensional world. It is not just a pleasing image to be glanced at from a distance, but something more in the nature of Marcel Duchamp's bottle-rack – a notorious piece of 'concrete art' of the twenties, of which it was once said, 'It is there to be used, ready for anything: it is alive. It lives on the fringe of existence its own disturbing, absurd life.'[12] The very existence of a mountain is a presence to be reckoned with. It is not just a visual treat, but a physical challenge.

Once we start to see mountains as three-dimensional natural sculptures we will not be satisfied just to look at them from a distance; to appreciate them fully we will need to explore them.

THE BASTEIR TOOTH SEEN FROM
BELOW

— 4 —
MOUNTAIN DREAMS AND REALITIES

A mountain is not an ancient, lifeless relic but a piece of living plastic art – put there, as it were, to be climbed. As a gigantic sculpture, it cannot avoid becoming woven around with climbing dreams.

AM BASTEIR AND THE BASTEIR TOOTH

THE COMPELLING LINE

A mountaineering challenge will not be of interest to a climber until he has a definite image of it in his mind, even if it is a false one. In fact, the aesthetic appeal of the proposed route is generally of far greater importance to him than the bald factual challenge of reaching the top – unless the mountain has never been climbed before. Far from simply being a matter of getting to the summit, the fascination of all forms of mountaineering, from easy hillwalking to extreme rockclimbing, lies in the quality and interest of the line taken – that is, the whole challenge the route presents from the bottom of the mountain to the top and not merely its end point. It has very little to do with statistics, such as the length of the route or the height the summit happens to be above sea level (though there is a curious breed of list-ticker who thinks otherwise – see Glossary: 'Munro-bagger').

THE BRISTLY RIDGE OF GLYDER FACH AT DUSK

That the interest of a mountaineering challenge depends largely on the aesthetic qualities of the route was first advanced by the great Victorian mountaineer, Alfred Frederick Mummery. If the summit is the only thing that is desired, he said, then the easiest way up is obviously the right way, 'but from a purely aesthetic standpoint' the harder ridges will provide a far richer experience.[13] In fact Mummery insisted that the aesthetic quality of the line was directly related to its difficulty, such that 'the more difficult an ascent, the bolder and more significant will usually be the immediate surroundings of the traveller.'

ON THE FINAL TOWERS OF THE MITRE RIDGE, GARBH CHOIRE, IN THE CAIRNGORMS

LEFT:
THE NORTH-EAST BUTTRESS OF BEN
NEVIS AT SUNRISE

THE SERPENTINE LINE OF THE
DEVIL'S RIDGE SEEN FROM SGURR A'
MHAIM

The greatest climbing lines – the ones which have the strongest hold on the imagination – are those that look both beautiful and awesomely impossible at the same time: 'sublime', that is, in the fullest, most paradoxical sense.

A bold line is not necessarily a simple one. Even the simplest looking lines are always much more complicated in close-up than they appear from a distance. It is this intricacy and complexity – the 'serpentine quality' that Hogarth spoke about – that gives a climbing route its uniqueness. Like a good melody or a good story, it is full of variety and unexpected twists and turns. The poet

FIRST SNOWS ON SPIDEAN
MIALACH, WESTERN HIGHLANDS

Gerard Manley Hopkins once compared the outline of a distant
hill to a 'slow tune';[14] and it was no doubt the strange power of
such a line, with its irresistible blend of bold simplicity and subtle
complexity, that led a famous 'climbing parson' in Snowdonia in
the 1840's to acquire an obsession for always 'following the skyline'
as closely as he could.[15]

A LONE CLIMBER ON THE NORTH-
EAST RIDGE OF SGOR BHAN, BEINN
A' BHEITHIR

RIGHT:
TRAVERSING THE DEVIL'S RIDGE
FROM SGOR AN IUBHAIR

A very complicated line can be as compelling as a simple one if it is the only solution to an obvious challenge. In fact, most long climbs are usually a clever linking together of several discontinuous natural weaknesses, with much less obvious sections in between. It is here that the pioneer's creative imagination is required; the image comes to mind of that great rockclimber of the 1930's, Colin Kirkus, cooped up all week in an office, pretending to work, but having the drawer of his desk slightly open so that he could see the photo of CLOGWYN D'UR ARDDU (*below*) on which he had drawn all the existing and possible routes with red lines.

JOHNNY DAWES ON 'WHITE SLAB' ON THE WEST BUTTRESS OF CLOGWYN D'UR ARDDU, SNOWDON

Perhaps it would not be too fanciful to say that climbing is like acting out an idea that has hitherto only existed on paper like the bare bones of a script; that an unclimbed mountain line is a storyline waiting to be enacted.

'*THE* PINNACLE, THE GREATEST PINNACLE, SURELY, IN THE WORLD – THE SCAFELL PINNACLE' (PAT KELLY)

LEFT:
DISTANT SGORR DHEARG (1024m)
SEEN FROM NEAR THE SUMMIT OF
BEN NEVIS

APPROACHING THE SUMMIT OF
SGORR DHEARG IN A STRONG WIND

ENTERING THE FORBIDDEN WORLD

The mountaineering spirit is one that wants to abolish completely the 'otherness' of the mountain world, to bridge the vast apparent gap between it and ourselves, to unmask the secret reality behind the dreamlike appearance. And it wants to do this, not by simply reducing the dream to the level of everyday reality, but by entering the dream like Alice in Wonderland. For it wants to leave everyday life behind and become, for a while, part of the 'other' – the world that civilised man shrinks from, and yet is irresistibly drawn to.

This romantic aspect of the mountains is reflected in some of the names given to the more inaccessible mountain features of Britain by Victorian climbers. The 'High Man' of Pillar Rock in the Lake District was actually called 'The Promised Land' by the early explorers, who could view it, like Moses, from an adjacent, easily accessible summit known as 'Pisgah' (from across a 'Jordan Gap'). Similarly, there was a Pisgah on Scafell from which the (then) unclimbed SCAFELL PINNACLE (*opposite*) could be viewed.

The romance of the inaccessible also carries with it a sense of the forbidden. The climber can never completely dispel a faint, nagging feeling that he ought not to be there, that this landscape was not really meant for man at all. Many inaccessible mountain features have been traditionally wrapped around with religious superstitions and taboos, and even in Britain there are a number of summits which were regarded until surprisingly recently as absolutely unclimbable; SGURR NAN GILLEAN (*below*), for example, was regarded as such until 1836.

SGURR NAN GILLEAN FROM THE
EAST AT DAWN

69

LEFT:
A LONE WALKER ON SCAFELL PIKE,
HIGH ABOVE ESKDALE, AT EASTER

THE 'INCREDIBLE SHRINKING MAN'

To enter the mountain world is to turn the two-dimensional world of distant appearances into a three-dimensional reality. It is the exact opposite of reducing the landscape to a small postcard view. For in this case it is the climber that becomes small – extremely small. The urge to enter right into the fabric of the landscape that has been called 'topophilia' – to understand all its inner secrets or, as Mummery said, to get to 'know every wrinkle'[16] – is to see the world as if through a powerful magnifying glass. A mountain feature, close-up, is as different – as beautifully different – as a geologist's rock-slide under the microscope. A smooth looking scree slope, for example, becomes more and more bumpy and three-dimensional, until it resolves itself into boulders the size of cars, and the walker finds himself not so much on it as in it. Once he is on the mountainside the climber has about as much understanding of the whole as an ant on the steps of St Paul's Cathedral.

STARTING THE 'MITRE RIDGE' ON
BEINN A' BHUIRD IN THE
CAIRNGORMS

PAGE 70:
SGURR FIONA (1059m), AN
TEALLACH, WESTER ROSS, NOT
CLIMBED UNTIL 1893

PAGE 71:
THE ICE-CLAD ORION FACE OF BEN
NEVIS IN MARCH. CLIMBERS CAN BE
SEEN NEAR THE TOP OF THE FACE
AND IN ZERO GULLY TO THE RIGHT

READING THE ROCK

To climb a mountain is to be let into a secret, but it is a secret that is revealed only to a few. The climber always has a sense of privilege; he has become part of an exclusive band of those who have gained access to the 'upper world', to use Mummery's term – a world that is only open to the few who are prepared to make the effort or take the risk.

The secret that the climber finds out is what the mountain is really made of, and just how much of an illusion it is. He alone discovers its true strengths and weaknesses. Nothing is as it appears from a distance. There is always so much more detail and texture – that is to say, potential holds – on a rock face, even on one that appears dauntingly smooth, than the layman realizes.

STARTING THE 'CNEIFION ARETE',
ABOVE CWM IDWAL, SNOWDONIA

MOVING ONTO EASY GROUND AT
THE TOP OF THE CRUX PITCH OF
'WEST FLANK ROUTE', CIR MHOR,
ARRAN

LEFT:
MOVING OUT ONTO THE CRUX OF
'MOSS LEDGE ROUTE' ON SCAFELL
PINNACLE

A STEEP SLAB ON THE 'CNEIFION ARETE'

BELOW:
TAKING CARE ON SLIMY, VEGETATED ROCK ON 'THE GREAT PITCH' OF THE DEVIL'S KITCHEN IN CWM IDWAL

W.H. Murray describes his discovery of the beautiful texture of rock on his first day's climbing: 'Always before I had thought of rock as a dull mass. But *this* rock was the living rock, pale grey and clean as the air itself, with streaks of shiny mica and white crystals of quartzite. It was a joy to handle such rock and to feel the coarse grain under the fingers.'[17]

Always in climbing there is a sense of grappling with the very stuff of the Earth, the lithosphere, on a one-to-one basis. Even if the particular piece of rock has been climbed many times before, providing it is not worn smooth, it feels just as if no one has ever touched it. Always there is the quiet, all-absorbing task of 'reading the rock', the intimate pleasure that Gaston Rébuffat talks about 'of communicating with the mountain . . . with its material self, its substance, as a craftsman communicates with the wood, the stone or the iron with which he is working. . . . To discover little hidden holds and, by means of them, an approach, a way through.'[18]

ROCK ARTISTRY

Until it is found, this 'way through' is like a puzzle that has had to wait thousands, if not millions of years to be solved, a secret that has lain dormant, waiting to be unlocked. And this is why the expression 'route *finding*' is so much more appropriate to climbing than 'route making' (or 'putting up a route', as some climbers will have it).

MOVING OUT OVER THE VOID ON 'AURA', ON THE AMPHITHEATRE WALL OF CRAIG YR YSFA

Certainly some climbs seem, like the mountains themselves, almost to have been *designed* – there are sequences of moves so subtle, so imaginative, so right, that even the cleverest inventor or most sophisticated computer programme could never have produced their equal.

Climbing is a playful game between the climber and the mountain – a creative interaction between a rock artiste (as we could call a top climber) and a natural art form. A climber can be seen as someone who enters right into the creative, playful spirit of nature. Often a climb displays a certain gamesmanship, even a sense of humour, in its ability to surprise or mislead. Sometimes I have made what I have thought are the hardest moves, been fooled, nearly fallen off, solved it – and, once over the difficulties, found myself chuckling in quiet appreciation at the sheer 'genius' of the climb.

The climber's enthusiasm for the genius of the rock – his topophilia – finds expression in the names he gives to the unique features of a climb: the Groves of Bollards and Rickety Innards, Droopy Flakes and Swords of Damocles, Man Traps and Obstretrician's Moves, Cracks of Doom and Amen Corners. (A personal favourite is 'the Quartz Babe'.) And the great climbs themselves: Cenotaph Corner, Cemetary Gates, the Footless Crow, the Indian Face – the list is endless.

No great climb ever resembles any other; it is something unique, having its own inimitable character and identity. Like Everest itself, once discovered, it can never be un-discovered. It is a permanent feature, accumulating its own unique history. JONES'S ROUTE DIRECT (*opposite*) on Scafell, for example, will be his for ever.

GRAPPLING WITH THE CRUX OF 'JONES'S ROUTE DIRECT' ON SCAFELL PINNACLE

SUPERMAN

THE INTIMIDATING ENTRY PITCH
OF 'THE GREAT PROW' ON BLA
BHEINN

Although a climber has to deal with the hard realities of a mountain, his experience of climbing it retains many of the qualities of a dream. Moving up steep rock or snow, in a 'world above the world' – with nothing but space behind and almost everything below – has an extraordinary, dreamlike quality that verges on magic. When he is climbing well, the climber feels as if he is floating in space, swimming upwards over overhangs like waves in a vertical sea, moving as it were in a new dimension, on the very edge of existence. This sensation of floating effortlessly, as in a dream, can be felt in all forms of climbing, even in strenuous hill walking (providing one is fit!) It is by far the most compelling reason why people climb: the magic feeling of fluidity, the sheer joy of movement.

Closely allied with this wonderful sensation of fluidity is the feeling, which many climbers have commented on, of extraordinary, unconquerable power – the sense, especially once the hardest moves are solved, that 'nothing can stop me now'.

BEN MOON ON 'JERRY'S ROOF', A
VERY STRENUOUS AND TECHNICAL
PROBLEM IN LLANBERIS PASS

LEFT:
ON THE CRUX OF 'AURA' ON THE
AMPHITHEATRE WALL, CRAIG YR
YSFA

TWO HUNDRED METRES OF AIR ON
'GREAT SLAB', CLOGWYN D'UR
ARDDU

At the same time, particularly on a very hard sequence of moves, the climber experiences a heightened awareness, with every faculty stretched to its limit, and everything in the immediate environment perceived with extraordinary vividness and intensity. It is not surprising that this effect, known in sports medicine as 'the Running High', should have something in common with the effects of drug-taking, for it is almost certainly the result of the production in the body of 'neurotransmitters' such as epinephrine (adrenaline) and endorphins, when it is *in extremis*. The fact that one may have this sensation while being in an outrageously beautiful or 'impossible' situation, poised on the edge of nothing in an extraordinary dream landscape, only adds to the overwhelmingly psychedelic quality of the experience.

COMPLETING THE 'CNEIFION
ARETE' ABOVE CWM IDWAL

BEYOND THE PLEASURE PRINCIPLE

It is often argued that such an extreme outdoor activity as
mountaineering, which seems to be motivated primarily by a
desire to get as far away as possible from ordinary experience, is
nothing more than escapism, or the search for pleasure. But
climbing is emphatically not just a matter of going out and
enjoying oneself. A mountain landscape, as we have seen, is one
that by its very nature stimulates a much broader and more
complex range of emotions than mere 'pleasure', and this is
therefore far too simplistic a term for the whole *sublime* complex
of emotions we feel when climbing. At its simplest, climbing
always involves a rather potent blend of exhilaration and fear. It is
worth remembering that the term 'pleasant' is generally used in
climbing guidebooks to suggest something rather tame and
undemanding – a climb that is almost by definition less than great.

DEHYDRATION ON THE CUILLIN
RIDGE IN MID-JUNE

Certainly climbing is not a lazy man's activity, as some have claimed. Even the approach walks to some climbs are arduous undertakings in their own right, and the vast majority of rock and ice routes, above a certain elementary level, are very strenuous by any standards. Indeed, climbing in general is, without question, one of the most strenuous sports there is. If it is a pleasure at all, it is a pleasure that, as Edward Whymper said long ago, is borne out of toil[19] – and often considerable hardship and very real danger. But, as Whymper insisted, 'out of the toil comes strength (not merely muscular energy – more than that), an awakening of all the faculties.'

Altogether more serious is the suggestion that climbing is an escape from reality. If we allow that movements towards or away from reality make any sense at all – I subscribe to precisely the opposite view: that climbing is actually a way of getting closer to reality, not only in the sense of coming face to face with some of the hardest and most fundamental realities of the inanimate world – of, as I have put it, grappling with the very stuff of the lithosphere – but also, by going to the boundaries of our own experience, of confronting some hard truths about ourselves, of discovering, perhaps, the limits of our courage and endurance. If we climbers have escaped from anything, it is from the essential unreality of the artificial 'space capsule' of modern existence. Instead, we have returned to a world that is entirely free of the wrappings of vainglory and pretension, and demands only that we should use all our faculties of perception and judgment as truly as possible.

COMPLETING THE 'GREAT PROW' ON BLA BHEINN, SEVEN HUNDRED AND FIFTY METRES ABOVE LOCH SLAPIN

PAGE 88/89:
CLASSIC ROCKCLIMBING IN THE LAKE DISTRICT: 'KIPLING GROOVE' ON GIMMER CRAG

— 5 —
MOUNTAIN IMAGES

THE GREAT MOUNTAIN TRENCH OF
GLENCOE, ARGYLL

AN IMPRINT OF NATURE

The great benefit of being able to take home some of our most
vivid landscape memories on film is that it enables us to appreciate
them more fully. With large format photography especially, we can
look even more closely at 'the given', and see much detail that we
did not notice at the time we took the picture.

RIGHT:
STOB COIRE NAN LOCHAN (1115m)

While the reduction of assorted landscape images onto relatively small sheets of paper, as in this book, admittedly excludes one of the key elements of the sublime, that of vastness, the eye is able to look at them all in the same way – whether they are extreme close-ups or extensive panoramas – with equal ease and clarity. We are left simply with the rich beauty of the thing itself.

ULLADALE RIVER, NORTH HARRIS.
THE BOAT HUT ON THE EDGE OF
LOCH ULLADALE GIVES THE SCALE

In fact, it is only once we start to look at nature in this rather detached and clinical manner that we can fully appreciate the French philosopher, Gaston Bachelard's dictum that 'macrocosm and microcosm are correlated'.[20] For although scale may be relevant to the sublime, it is of no relevance whatever to the beautiful. As Bachelard expresses it: 'If a poet looks through a microscope or a telescope, he always sees the same thing.'[21]

A TWO-METRE HIGH OUTCROP IN RUTHWAITE COVE, CUMBRIA

PINNACLE WALL ON CRAIG YR YSFA, SNOWDONIA

The scale of inanimate natural objects is an entirely human, or animal, concern. It has no bearing whatever on their complexity. A mountain ridge is just as intricate in close-up as it is on a much larger scale; indeed the close-up often mimics the more distant view. Modern scientists interested in the irregular patterns of nature have called this principle, which is seen in operation throughout the inanimate world, 'self-similarity'.

'SELF-SIMILARITY' ON THE CUILLIN RIDGE, SKYE. THE NORTHERN END OF THE MAIN RIDGE AS SEEN FROM SGURR DUBH NA DA BHEINN

THE PARTICULARITY OF THE MOMENT

The photographer's main interest cannot, however, simply be in recording 'slices of nature' in this way – in taking home what amounts to samples for further study. For the essence of photography resides entirely in the particularities of a moment. Rather than taking bland, generalised, timeless images as a record of physical geography, the photographer tries to convey something of the landscape's impact on him at a certain moment so that others may appreciate it in much the same way as he did.

Everything about an extraordinary moment of this kind is by nature a surprise; and its particularity is such that it can never recur in precisely the same way again – just as the landscape photograph that has captured this quality can never be repeated.

RIGHT:
THE VIEW WEST FROM THE SUMMIT OF SGURR NAN GILLEAN TOWARDS AM BASTEIR

SGURR A' FIONN CHOIRE AND AM BASTEIR, CUILLIN MAIN RIDGE

*To see them is worth a week's
waiting – to see the black peaks
start out like living creatures,
high above the clouds which
wildly career up the cleft ridges,
now hiding and now revealing
their awful faces, or calmly
rising, like the spires and towers
of a celestial city, out of a
snowy sea of mist . . .*

ALEXANDER NICOLSON
(1875)

It is absolutely unique. Or, to put it the other way round: to the extent that it *can* be repeated, it is ordinary and lacks memorability. It doesn't do anything except record a view: that is, show how the scene 'normally' looks from such and such a viewpoint at a certain time of year.

Closely connected with this generalising, timeless conception of landscape photography is the fallacious idea that there is such a thing as the 'spirit' of a place and that the photographer's main purpose is to try and capture this on one frame of film. It is certainly true that any mountain area has its own special characteristics that can be summarised and encapsulated in a photograph in a very vague and general way, but its overriding quality is always its essential changeability.

This was the point those early visitors to LOCH CORUISK (*p.14*) missed completely. They made the fundamental mistake – as extraordinary as it was illogical, given their knowledge of the British weather – of assuming that a mountain scene is always the same, ever of one mood. Whereas, what any seasoned traveller will know is that it will appear entirely different on different occasions, depending on when he happens to see it, what part of it he happens to see, and his own particular mood at the time.

The tendency to generalise – which is a barrier to all true appreciation – remains an extremely common one. There are many people, for example, who seriously believe that it always rains in the Cuillins, or who do not like Llanberis Pass or GLENCOE (*p.92*) because they are 'dark and forbidding'. I am sure many of them would be amazed to see just how different these places look under the mantle of winter snow. SNOWDON itself is transformed into a majestic white cone that bears a distinct resemblance to Mount Everest in miniature (*pp.125, 127*).

BAOSBHEINN – 'THE WIZARD'S
MOUNTAIN' – WESTER ROSS

The true character of a landscape, through time, can only be conveyed by a portfolio of photographs that try to show all its typical and changing aspects – just as the real character of a person can only be discerned by observing his or her actions and moods at a wide range of different moments. The mountain photographer will want to see a landscape in as many different guises as possible, appreciating that they all have their own distinctive appeal. His special craft is to see always what is *different* around him, to see the world as something that is continuously changing and new, and to see it with fresh eyes. To see it always in a new light.

CRIB GOCH (921m), SNOWDONIA, FROM BELOW BWLCH COCH

THE SAME VIEWPOINT, A WEEK LATER, IN A BLIZZARD

RIGHT:
CRIB GOCH AND LLYN GLAS IN THE GRIP OF LATE WINTER SNOW

RANNOCH MOOR AFTER A
SNOWSTORM. THE MOUNTAINS ARE
STOB A' GHLAIS CHOIRE (996m) AND
BUACHAILLE ETIVE MOR (1022m)

LET THERE BE LIGHT

UNEXPECTED LIGHT ON LOCH
COIRE NAN ARR IN WESTER ROSS

It is the quality of light, above all else, that makes a 'landscape moment' special. Fortunately for the photographer this is the one quality that his medium is uniquely and precisely able to record.

If we accept that the weather and light are part of a landscape, we will be as interested in the quality of the light as in the physical geography of the scene. Interesting topography is not enough. The photographer may have all the physical ingredients for the image he desires, but if he has not got interesting light he has got nothing – or, at most, something that is entirely unremarkable. Much of the visual potential of the landform will lie dormant; the surface will be dead, at rest, sleeping.

By the 'quality of light' I mean, of course, the whole colour spectrum and not just its monochromatic qualities of intensity and diffusion. The human eye is in fact very lazy when it comes to seeing the full richness and subtlety of natural colour, particularly in poor light when its black and white-sensitive 'rods' assume a greater importance than its colour sensitive 'cones'. In such conditions it is only by making a very conscious effort that we may notice any colour content at all.

A STREAM HIGH ON THE SOUTH
FLANK OF FUAR THOLL, WESTER
ROSS

PAGE 106:
BEINN A' MHUINIDH WATERFALL,
WESTER ROSS, IN THE AUTUMN

PAGE 107:
ROWAN TREE BESIDE ABHAINN AN
FHASHAIGH, KINLOCHEWE FOREST,
WESTER ROSS

Landscape photography at its purest requires nothing more to be happening in the scene than the quality of light to be changing in an interesting way. And the most striking photographs of all occur when the light itself becomes an *event*.

BUTTERMERE IN THE AUTUMN

108

THE QUEST FOR THE DREAM IMAGE

Special moments of extraordinary light are not something that the photographer can ever plan for; he has to content himself with chasing dream images of his own. In photography, as in climbing: first we have a dream, then we try to turn it into a reality. Only, for the mountain photographer, the dream image itself becomes the goal. He wants to fix it on a piece of paper for posterity. Ideally, he wants to produce the sort of photographs that Roland Barthes has called 'fantasmatic', which have the capacity to connect with a world that somehow already exists in the viewer's imagination.[22] The landscape becomes something we want to enter; in our imagination, we in effect get right into the photograph. Such a photo no longer remains a small, fuzzy image in a book or a photo album, but becomes an enormous, mind-filling potentiality that can no longer be contained by a little rectangular frame.

Although the photographer may not always have a vivid, well-defined image in his mind's eye, the dream image he chases after must always be sketchable, in some form or other. For, until he has such a clear visual concept he will have little chance of obtaining it. He will then be in the position of the famous mathematician who once said that he had had his solutions for a long time, but did not yet know how he would arrive at them.

ROUGH SKETCH OF A PLANNED
DOUBLE-PAGE SPREAD OF
SNOWDON

LEFT:
THE WESTERN MAMORES FROM
SGURR A' MHAIM

THE CONQUEST OF SPACE

Just as we cannot see a mountain landscape properly except by becoming physically involved in it, so the process of hunting down our mountain dream images is unavoidably a very physical one too. The fact is that many of the major mountain features of Britain are not visible from any road, and cannot be reached without considerable effort. Some form of climbing, if only in the sense of uphill walking, is almost always necessary. It seems that beauty in mountain photography – like pleasure in mountaineering – only comes out of toil. There are always, as it were, major strings attached in the form of physical effort and discomfort – and sometimes no strings at all, when what is most needed for peace of mind or even safety is a substantial climbing rope.

DESCENDING INTO CWM UCHAF,
SNOWDONIA, AT DUSK

Long days are the norm for the mountain photographer, whose lot is to spend hours wading through deep powder snow, or teetering down icy rocks in crampons with a heavy sack, or toiling up scree slopes under the blazing sun. But grand as it may sound, the aim is to conquer space – to levitate the camera so that it is no longer obviously earthbound but more in the nature of a disembodied flying eye that can look in on the beauty of the lithosphere from wherever it wishes. The existence of the photographer must be nowhere in evidence; the eye of the dream must have complete autonomy.

PAGE 112/113:
LIATHACH (1054m) FROM BEINN
EIGHE

*. . . A chain of rocky mountains with sides dark, deep and
precipitous; with summits broken, sharp, and serrated, and
springing into all terrific forms; with snowy glaciers lodged in the
deep shaded apertures . . .*

THOMAS PENNANT'S DESCRIPTION OF AN
TEALLACH IN 1772

Ben moon dwarfed by the
North-west face of Strone
Ulladale, North Harris

THE RIGHT PLACE AT THE RIGHT TIME

'To be in the right place at the right time' is an obvious truism, but it is the key to landscape photography. It is probably best re-expressed by using the concept of 'ripeness': the time must be ripe, and the photographer must be ready, if the hoped-for image is to be recorded on film. It is extremely unlikely, for example, that a picture of a climber on a remote, outlandish mountain feature like STRONE ULLADALE (*opposite*) will be obtained in interesting light by accident. Even for the time to be ripe – that is, for the photographer simply to be there in fine weather at a favourable time of year – is not enough: as many favourable circumstances as possible have to be organized and brought together. The riper the whole situation, the less need there is to rely on chance.

The first requirement, in Britain's predominantly cyclonic climate, is to try to get 'in phase with' the weather – that is, to try and organize one's shoots so that they coincide with any ridges of high pressure that may occur. This may mean, for example, having to go up to a high camp in the rain if the forecast is good in order to catch a 'window' of fine weather the moment it arrives.

But of course it is no good if the whole situation is ripe and the photographer is not ready. In medium and large format photography, it is not just a matter of having the camera loaded and wound on to the first frame; the shutter must be cocked, the dark slide extracted, and the aperture must be readjusted manually as every change of light is monitored with a separate meter. Only in this state of readiness can the photographer respond quickly to the unexpected.

To have the camera all ready in position with time to spare – at dawn, for example, after a long and difficult approach walk in the dark – is immensely satisfying. Equally, there are few experiences more mortifying in mountain photography than being just too late, for a magic moment never repeats itself. Indeed, catching the landscape at exactly the right moment is no less an act of precision than catching the most vivid expression in a person's face. It must be caught immediately, for it will be gone in a millisecond. The perception that a scene has 'lost something' will always be borne out when the transparencies are projected in quick succession at home. But it is equally important, when using a large format 'view camera' – which cannot immediately be advanced to a new frame – not to be overhasty and take it too soon, for a magic moment always 'peaks out'. Ripeness is all.

SIDE PIKE, LANGDALE, IN THE AUTUMN

PAGE 122/123:
BUACHAILLE ETIVE MOR AT SUNRISE

SNOWDON EMERGES FROM THE
CLOUD

IMPROVING WEATHER OVER
LLANBERIS PASS

THE STUFF OF DREAMS

Despite all the effort and patience that goes into obtaining a
'fantasmatic' image, it is still something of a shock when it
suddenly materialises in front of the photographer's very eyes.
Several times, in taking the photographs for this book, I have had
the extraordinary experience of finding myself looking straight at
an image that has existed up till then only in my imagination. But
it has acquired such a powerful place in my mind that I am then
truly in the state described by Novalis when 'dream becomes
world, world becomes dream'.[23]

124

These mountains may not unfitly be termed the British Alpes, as being the most vaste of all Britain . . . all of them towering up into the aire, and round encompassing one farre higher than alle the rest, peculiarly called Snowdon-Hill . . . for all the year long these lye mantelled over with snow hard crusted together.

JOHN SPEED (1610)

CRIB GOCH, SNOWDON AND CRIB Y DDYSGL FROM ACROSS LLANBERIS PASS

LEFT:
RAIN SWEEPS UP LOCH MAREE IN
NOVEMBER

NO SHORTCUTS OR TRICKS

In spite of all his efforts, the photographer is always ultimately at the mercy of chance. There are periods when the gods seem to smile, and periods when nothing seems to work out as planned. There is no magic formula beyond patience and persistence, particularly as only about one day in five in the British mountains will provide moments of real photographic merit, while on at least two of those five days almost nothing of value will be obtained.

And so hours and days will be spent walking and watching and waiting, often with the camera covered with a polythene bag to keep out the rain; but one must never lose patience, for it is just when one starts to put the camera away that one's luck is most likely to change.

RAINBOW OVER LOCH MAREE

What one must never do is resort to gimmickry – such as coloured filters or double exposures – in the attempt to construct a shot out of nothing. For one is likely to become so engrossed in one's own 'creativity' that the magic moment, when it does occur, may be missed; one may not even *see* it. If a scene is of so little intrinsic merit, or the light is so dull, that it requires such tricks, nothing will save it. Magic cannot be superimposed from outside.

We do not need tricks in mountain photography. All we need is what we already have – the magic of nature and the film emulsion.

RIGHT:
DUSK OVER LOCH HARPORT, FROM THE SUMMIT OF SGURR A' FIONN CHOIRE ON THE CUILLIN RIDGE

CUL MOR FROM SUILVEN AT SUNSET

I saw in the eternal evening
glow the silent world at my feet.
Every height on fire, every
valley at rest, the silver brook
flowing into the golden stream.
GOETHE

*The sun rose on the flawless
brimming sea into a sky all
brazen.*

ODYSSEY (III: 1–2)

Tr. Fitzgerald

SUNRISE BEHIND THE BASTEIR
TOOTH, CUILLIN RIDGE

THE MAGIC OF THE MEDIUM

It is indeed all too easy when emphasising the importance in
mountain photography of interesting light and topography to forget
the magical contribution of the film medium itself.

Even the most experienced photographer will readily admit that
his results are always different, even if in some very subtle way,
from what he expected. Because the camera and the film, by their
very nature, see the scene in a different way from the eye, the
photograph will always *add* something of its own – if only in the

sense of those special qualities such as colour saturation and grain that are inherent in the photographic emulsion. It is extremely difficult for the photographer to assess precisely how the very sensitive sheet of film in the camera – kept until then entirely in the dark – is going to register that sudden finely focussed flash of light from the outside world. The photographer is in every sense a bystander, a solicitous outsider who simply sets the process in motion and then has to wait and see.

This will not be seen as a shortcoming once we come to realize that this is precisely where the true magic of photography lies. For, just as there will be frequent disappointments, there will be occasions when we will be quite frankly amazed how unexpectedly beautiful a picture turns out – or, if we are honest with ourselves – just how exquisitely *different* it is from the way that we intended.

It is as if, at times, this particular fortuity of light and this particular sheet of film emulsion have joined forces in some kind of holy alliance – a sort of photographic alchemy – to produce an image that is aglow forever with the wonder of the moment. How right Roland Barthes was to call photography 'a magic, not an art'![24]

'THE GREAT PROW' OF BLA BHEINN CATCHES THE LAST RAYS OF THE SUN

EARLY MORNING ON THE CARN
MOR DEARG ARETE: THE NORTH-
EAST BUTTRESS OF BEN NEVIS, WITH
CARN DEARG MEADHONACH
BEHIND

PAGE 136/137:

THE PANORAMA TO THE SOUTH:
STOB COIRE A' CHAIRN, AM
BODACH AND SGURR A' MHAIM

RIGHT:

SIXTY KILOMETRES AWAY TO THE
EAST, SCHIEHALLION (1083m) RISES
ABOVE A SEA OF CLOUD

All southward the valleys brimmed with cloud, from which the tips of high peaks projected like skerries . . . On the broad snow-fields beneath our boots each crystal crumb threw its own shadow on to the gleaming crust. The whole frozen world was alive with the shining of light.

W. H. MURRAY (1951)

— 6 —
MOUNTAIN FRIENDS AND FOES

Such a view produces the powerful but shadowy impression one expects from an opium dream. The vast perspective drags itself out to a horizon so distant as to blend imperceptibly with the lower sky. It has the vague suggestion of rhythmical motion, strangely combined with eternal calm.

LESLIE STEPHEN (1894)

THE VIEW WEST FROM SRON NA CICHE ON THE ISLE OF SKYE, AT SUNSET

THE EAST FACE OF TRYFAN AT
SUNRISE

OUR APPRECIATION OF MOUNTAINS

I am always suspicious of people who say they *love* mountains. Genuine admirers of mountain scenery usually regard it with a rather ambivalent mixture of wonder and awe, which can degenerate, at times, into straightforward fear and loathing. But such forced sentimentality for these cold, unforgiving objects is all part of what one might call the consumer-package approach to landscape which derives from the 'glorious scenery' language of travel brochures. It leads to an inevitable blunting of our powers of perception. We tend only to see a view as very obviously 'beautiful' – or not at all. We react as we are expected to react; we have little time for our own feelings, or taste for subtleties. While any redder-than-average sunset provokes an entirely predictable, almost Pavlovian response of 'oohs' and 'aahs' from us, we are unlikely to dwell on it for more than a few seconds – let alone to witness the whole wonder of the transition from day to night.

LOOKING UP LOCH ETIVE TOWARDS
THE DISTANT MOUNTAINS OF
GLENCOE, LATE EVENING

THE SAME, AT DUSK

Another common form of exaggeration is to call any unremarkable rounded hill a 'peak', or any steep, loose slope a 'sheer cliff'. The truth is that there are as many different types of mountain as there are people – all the way from the eminent, the elegant, and the forbidding, through the undistinguished and the nondescript, to those that are just plain ugly.

Ruskin, a most enthusiastic admirer of mountain scenery, was still capable of describing a scene in the Alps as a 'smooth, slippery, glutinous heap, looking like a beach of black scales of dead fish, cast ashore from a poisonous sea. . . .'[25] We too must not be afraid of calling some mountains ugly. We have to learn to differentiate, for example, the shapeless rottenness of Red Pike in the Lake District, or the Red Cuillins in Skye, from the nearby splendours of Pillar Rock and the Black Cuillins, respectively. One of the Red Cuillins, Glamaig, has been described as a 'graceful cone' when in reality it is the epitome of a slag heap – its obvious rottenness only accentuated by its unfortunate proximity to the solid grandeur of SGURR NAN GILLEAN (*below*). We need to distinguish the good, the bad, and the ugly when it comes to rock types. It is, indeed, an old adage of mine that where there is good rock for climbing there is a fine landscape – that the most aesthetically pleasing mountains are those that are made of the best rock.

SGURR NAN GILLEAN FROM THE WEST

Only once we have learnt to look more critically at landscapes will we be able to see that much that initially appears ugly contains unexpected beauties, which cannot be entirely separated from their ugliness. Appreciating these subtleties demands more than just using the eyes better; it involves the application of the whole intellect. As the artist John Constable said, 'the art of seeing nature is a thing almost as much to be acquired as the art of reading Egyptian hieroglyphs.'[26]

A MOSSY STREAM HIGH ON FUAR THOLL, WESTER ROSS

POINT-SCORING

One of the problems that the 'consumer boom' has brought with it
is a shift in the values of those who visit the hills. Everywhere, it
seems, there is an urge to turn the quality of the mountain
experience into something quantifiable – not just in terms of height
above sea level or mileage, but in terms of gradable achievement,
so that it is all conformable and comparable with what other
people are doing or have done. Everywhere, whole days are
reduced to grades and numbers so that they are, in effect, given a
score – the 'success' of hillwalking days being measured by the
number of Munros climbed, and rockclimbing days (since the
subdivision of the Extreme grade into E numbers) by the number
of 'E points' gained. (See Glossary: E points.)

SPRING SNOW ON GARBH BHEINN
(885m), ARDGOUR
. . . NOT A 'MUNRO'

For a mountaineering day to be judged a 'success' is nothing to do with success in the ordinary sense of the word. The only relevant sense of 'winning' in the mountains is that we win through, and this often means having to let the mountain 'win'. The clichéd idea, often heard in the media, of 'conquering' a mountain is a popular misconception: the idea that a mountain is an anthropomorphic opponent that we must crush – or it will crush us.

COIRE LAGAN, ISLE OF SKYE, IN THE LATE EVENING

STRIDING EDGE, HELVELLYN, ON A
BANK HOLIDAY

Once walking or climbing days are judged solely by their
Munro-bagging or E-point productivity, they are reduced almost to
the status of a job, to a repetitive routine that has been stripped of
much of its meaning and adventure. More and more it is just a
matter of another path to be followed, another well-worn script to
be repeated. More and more the mountain day mimics, in a sort of
grotesque ritual, the treadmill of everyday life, as a seemingly
endless stream of walkers tramp along STRIDING EDGE (*above*) or
around such contrivances as the 'Buttermere Circuit' – which has
the 'advantage' of providing more 'peaks' (protuberances) to be
'bagged', with only little more effort.

It seems to me that this approach to days in the mountains limits
much of their potential for real adventure. The point of an
adventure is that we can never have any clear idea of its storyline
in advance; it always takes us somewhere new; and it always
follows a complex, serpentine line, full of surprising twists and
turns, some very abrupt. It is never a simple movement from A to
B, but a journey in many dimensions: it opens up a whole new
realm of experience.

RIGHT:
'BELLE VUE BASTION' ON THE EAST
FACE OF TRYFAN

The quality of a mountain day depends largely on how interesting its *shape* is, how far out of the ordinary its storyline, and how intensely its extraordinariness is felt. By embarking on such adventures we give a meaning and a shape to our lives; by reacting creatively to the structure of the mountains themselves we re-create ourselves.

LEFT:
A VIEW OF THE LONELY VALLEY OF ENNERDALE, WHICH CANNOT BE SEEN FROM THE 'BUTTERMERE CIRCUIT' A HUNDRED OR SO METRES ABOVE

SUPERB WINTER HILLWALKING ON SGURR A' MHAIM IN THE MAMORES

THE SCOURGE OF 'DEVELOPMENT'

Unfortunately, a great deal of what goes under the name of 'development' – an appalling misnomer when applied to our wilder mountain areas – panders directly to the point-scoring, route-ticking mentality. All too often we find that, in addition to walks to be 'done' and peaks to be 'bagged', there are a host of other 'attractions' to be enjoyed: improved access roads to be followed, wonders of civil engineering to be admired, signposts to be obeyed, noticeboards to be read, dotted lines to be followed, souvenirs to be bought, and litter bins to be emptied by someone else.

Once an unspoilt area has been 'opened up' in this way – that is to say, been *spoiled* – it can never be unspoiled again. As a genuinely wild area it has been lost for ever.

It is true that we are faced with a major dilemma when it comes to the upkeep and repair of mountain paths, given the ever-increasing number of people visiting the hills. But it seems to me that the blasting of rock and the proliferation of unwarranted signs are clear-cut examples of over-zealous 'improvement'.

THE 'ZIG-ZAGS' ON THE PIG TRACK, SNOWDON

But before we start pointing accusing fingers at the developers we would do well, as walkers and climbers, to put our own house in order first. The pressures on the mountain environment in Britain are now so intense that we need to state unequivocally what has long been a vague unwritten law: that in walking and climbing in the hills we should leave everything exactly as we found it, and that we should regard any recreation or sporting activity which entails modifying the structure of the earth – the surface of the lithosphere – in whatever way, as an act of vandalism.

In rockclimbing, there has been a recent outbreak of 'hold-chipping', which has ranged all the way from over-enthusiastic 'cleaning' and 'improving' to the wholesale construction of new holds with a chisel. Which is roughly equivalent, in my mind, to taking a sledge-hammer to Michelangelo's David or slashing the face of the Mona Lisa with a knife.

LOOKING TOWARDS SGURR ALASDAIR FROM THE INACCESSIBLE PINNACLE, ON THE ISLE OF SKYE

MINDLESS WALKING

RIGHT:
GREAT MOSS, UPPER ESKDALE,
CUMBRIA

In walking, the damage that is done is far less deliberate, but that in a way is the problem: people pay far too little attention to where and how they walk – about what they put their feet into and onto, and how carefully.

Recently, on a path below the Cobbler, I encountered a boggy section which had all the appearance of an army of a thousand having marched straight across it, thirty abreast, without looking to right or to left. My disgust at this particular example of mindlessness was all the greater when I discovered that, without being particularly clever, it was possible to cross the bog by stepping from one embedded stone to another without putting one's foot into it once.

Sadly, there is nothing at all unusual about this unnecessary damage; such unintelligent footprints can be seen all over the British hills today. Perhaps the time has come for us to take Edward Whymper's famous words 'look well to each step'[27] in a broader sense, and ensure that we tread more carefully, treating each foot placement as precisely as if it were a foothold on a potentially dangerous climb – and let the lack of noise we make and the absence of any damage we leave be a testimony of our love of the landscape, and of our worthiness to be in it.

NORMAN CROUCHER STARTING UP
CRIB GOCH – WITH TWO ARTIFICIAL
LEGS AND A PAIR OF CRUTCHES

A MIRROR OF OUR WISDOM

BEINN DEARG MHOR, WESTER ROSS, AT DAWN

We must look after the surface of the planet, not just for material reasons, but because it mirrors our whole spiritual being. Just as the way we look after our homes is a reflection of our inner selves, so the way we treat our wilderness areas and national parks is a reflection of our national state of health.

The landscape is a mirror of our wisdom or our lack of it. If we spoil it, we must accept that it is because we ourselves are spoiled. If we destroy it, it means nothing less than that we have lost the fight against our own folly.

When we look at a so-called development area in our mountains we have to ask ourselves whether it is a true reflection of ourselves, and whether it reflects us in the way we would like. Are we proud, for example, of the ski development in the Cairngorms? Or are we embarrassed that so many wild places reveal us to be merely consumers and despoilers?

Our appreciation of anything and everything in the world starts with a respect for the ground beneath our feet, the living rock. If we cannot appreciate the most basic material of the planet, what hope is there for the higher forms of life? If we cannot refrain from vandalizing the solid structure of the lithosphere, how much worse will be the havoc we wreak upon the fragility of the biosphere? The relation between the two is a very close one – we cannot separate them; and we are part of it all.

The sea itself, though it can be clear, is never calm in the sense that a mountain lake can be calm. The sea seems only to pause; the mountain lake to sleep, and to dream.

JOHN RUSKIN (1856)

WINTRY WILDERNESS ON MEALL A'
MHUTHAICH NEAR SUILVEN

AN OMINOUS CLOUD OVER STAC
POLLAIDH AT DUSK

NORMAN CROUCHER TRAVERSING
CRIB GOCH

AN ADVENTURE PLAYGROUND

Through exploring mountains and climbing rocks, man comes into
a very special relationship with the raw material of the
lithosphere; by working out the problems posed by these natural
forms, the human spirit – essentially a spirit of exploration and
play, curiosity and cunning – comes into direct contact with the
'genius' of the rock. Here, where the earth's surface has been
thrown up and laid bare in enormous three-dimensional sculptures
of great variety and complexity, is to be found the supreme
landscape of adventure, a playground *par excellence* for the whole
superfluity of the human spirit.

A real mountain adventure, by which I mean anything from
serious mountain walking to extreme rock or ice climbing in a
mountain terrain (above *or* below 3000 feet), is the very opposite
of an organised 'game', whose lifeline is the rulebook. When we
are genuinely at play, that is to say, apparently playing around, or
playing the fool, essentially what we are doing is getting to know
more about our immediate environment by playing in it and
experimenting with it, as a child does. And because this demands a
spontaneous, improvisatory approach, it virtually necessitates the
breaking of rules.

RIGHT:
NAPES NEEDLE ON GREAT GABLE,
HIGH ABOVE WASDALE

It does not, however, mean treating the environment as a playground, in the everyday sense of the word. This is a serious game because it is a potentially dangerous game; it involves a dangerous propinquity with the elements and, as such, demands our greatest respect.

But nor is it the perverse kind of game – which has been called 'deep play' – that deliberately dices with death. Though most climbers have at some time or other got themselves into a situation where their very lives have hung in the balance, this can never be said to be their *motive* for going to the mountains.

We go to the mountains not as reckless stuntmen, as dicers with death, but as prospectors of life. Any risks we take are carefully calculated ones in which the real danger to life is reduced as far as possible. We want to return at the end of the day. If we are right to say that a great day's climbing has the completeness of a good story or a piece of music, then we are not interested in unfinished symphonies.

Unlike a game, in which we want to conquer our opponent and improve our position in the league table, climbing is an adventure in which we do not want to conquer or change anything. We do not want to damage either ourselves or the environment; we want to leave everything exactly as it is. A game is something we are said to play, but it is pursued in a spirit of aggression; an adventure involves real danger, but is pursued in a spirit of play. And it is this ever-present duality of genuine play and genuine risk, of lightheartedness and seriousness, that is the overriding characteristic of the mountain adventure.

LEFT:
A CLIMBER SOLOING 'OUTSIDE EDGE ROUTE' ON CRAIG YR OGOF IN SNOWDONIA

NORMAN CROUCHER ENJOYING THE VIEW ON CRIB GOCH

HIGH SPIRITS ON SCAFELL PIKE

FRIENDS OF THE MOUNTAINS

Those who come to the mountain landscape in this playful, adventurous, nature-loving spirit are a part of what gives it life. It could almost be said that, for a time, they belong to it. And because the mountain landscape attracts like minds, they will meet many of the same spirit who are in harmony with each other no less than with their surroundings. As Don Whillans said: 'The climb isn't the main thing, it's only half of it. The rest is being in the mountains and the company that I'm with.'[28]

The company of mountaineers and rockclimbers – which we may perhaps call 'the fraternity of the rock' – is a completely open society. International in spirit, contemptuous of all boundaries, indifferent to all considerations of status or background, nationality or wealth, it is open to all who treat the mountain environment with respect.

BEN MOON AND JOHNNY DAWES
AFTER A FIRST ASCENT ON STRONE
ULLADALE

LEFT:
THE 'INACCESSIBLE PINNACLE',
SGURR DEARG

In entering the mountain world there is always a sense of returning home, to something very old that is in danger of being forgotten, to a world of no nonsense or artifice, peopled by an extraordinary assortment of cool-headed and warm-hearted individuals who are as sound as the rock itself. A world whose simple pleasures and playful adventures spring directly from a deep appreciation of all that really matters, which is based at heart on a deep appreciation of nature.

Like Ruskin, I believe that this love of nature, or 'landscape instinct', as he called it, is totally inconsistent with 'all care, hatred, anxiety, and moroseness'.[29] The high hills promote high spirits and good feelings towards each other. They enlarge and strengthen us. However often we join them, we will never tire of them. However familiar they become, they will always provide us with something new. They give us a rich succession of memorable days, that runs through our lives like an unfolding dream.

ACROSS THE 'GREY CORRIES' TO BEN NEVIS FROM STOB CHOIRE CLAURIGH

PAGE 170/171:
CRIB GOCH, SNOWDON, AND CRIB Y DDYSGL FROM THE NORTH-EAST

In these two eyes
that search the splendour of the earth, and seek
the sombre mysteries on plain and peak,
all vision wakes and dies.
With these my ears
that listen for the sound of lakes asleep
and love the larger rumour from the deep,
the eternal hears:–
    For all of beauty that this life can give
        lives only while I live;
    and with the light my hurried vision lends
        all beauty ends.

GEOFFREY WINTHROP YOUNG

LLANBERIS PASS AT SUNSET

REFERENCES

1 From a 'famous Letter' by a Dr Brown, quoted by W.P. Haskett Smith, *Climbing in the British Isles* (Glasgow, 1986), p.77.

2 Walter Scott, 1814. Quoted in Derek Cooper, *Skye* (London, 1989), p.177.

3 John MacCulloch, 1819. Ibid., p.173.

4 James Wilson, 1842. Ibid., p.38.

5 Edmund Burke, *A Philosophical Enquiry into . . . the Sublime and the Beautiful* (Oxford, 1987), pp.136, 73.

6 Ibid., p.57.

7 J.M. Edwards, 'A Great Effort' (*Climbers' Club Journal*, 1941).

8 Leslie Stephen, *The Playground of Europe* (London, 1894), p.281.

9 John Ruskin, *Modern Painters*, Vol.III (London, 1856), Ch.XII 'Of the Pathetic Fallacy'.

10 R.L.G. Irving, *Alpine Journal*, xlix, p.164.

11 William Hogarth, *Analysis of Beauty* (London, 1753), p.25.

12 Jean Bazaine, quoted in *Man and his Symbols*, ed. Carl Jung (London, 1978), p.290.

13 A.F. Mummery, *My Climbs in the Alps and Caucasus* (Oxford, 1936), pp.97–8.

14 W.H. Gardner, *Poems and Prose of Gerard Manley Hopkins* (London, 1953), p.xx.

15 W.P. Haskett Smith, *Climbing in the British Isles* (Glasgow, 1986), p.12. 'His name I could never learn.'

16 Mummery, ibid., p.2.

17 W.H. Murray, *Undiscovered Scotland* (London, 1951), pp.2–3.

18 Gaston Rébuffat, *On Snow and Rock* (London, 1963), pp.19–20.

19 Edward Whymper, *Scrambles amongst the Alps* (London, 1871), p.333.

20 Gaston Bachelard, *The Poetics of Space* (Boston, 1969), p.170.

21 Ibid., p.172.

22 Roland Barthes, *Camera Lucida* (London, 1984), p.40.

23 Quoted in Roger Cardinal, *German Romantics in Context* (London, 1975), p.150.

24 Barthes, ibid., p.88.

25 John Ruskin, *Modern Painters*, Vol.IV (London, 1856), Ch.X 'Of the Materials of Mountains', p.119.

26 Quoted in Arthur Koestler, *The Act of Creation* (London, 1970), p.378.

27 Whymper, ibid., p.334.

28 Adrian Bailey, *Lakeland Rock* (London, 1985), p.67.

29 John Ruskin, *Modern Painters*, Vol.III (London, 1856), Ch.XVII 'The Moral of Landscape'.

GLOSSARY

CRUX   The hardest part of a climb, or of a section of a climb, usually consisting of a sequence of hard moves.

E POINTS   A system used by some climbers whereby the success of a day's climbing is measured by the aggregate grade of the Extreme routes climbed. E.g. one E4, two E3's, and one E2 will give a score of twelve 'E points'.
(See also 'British Rockclimbing Grades', below.)

MUNRO   A summit in the British Isles that exceeds 3,000 feet above sea level. Named after Hugh T. Munro who, in 1891, first listed all the 3,000 foot peaks in Scotland, and classified them into 'tops' and 'mountains'.

MUNRO-BAGGER   A hillwalker who is only interested in climbing Munros, the ultimate aim being to climb all 603 such tops in Britain and Ireland.

BRITISH ROCKCLIMBING GRADES

In ascending order of difficulty:
Moderate, Difficult (Diff), Very Difficult (V.Diff), Severe, Very Severe (V.S.), Hard Very Severe (Hard V.S.), and Extremely Severe, which is now itself divided into E1 to E9. (Before 1970, the top standard was about E3.)

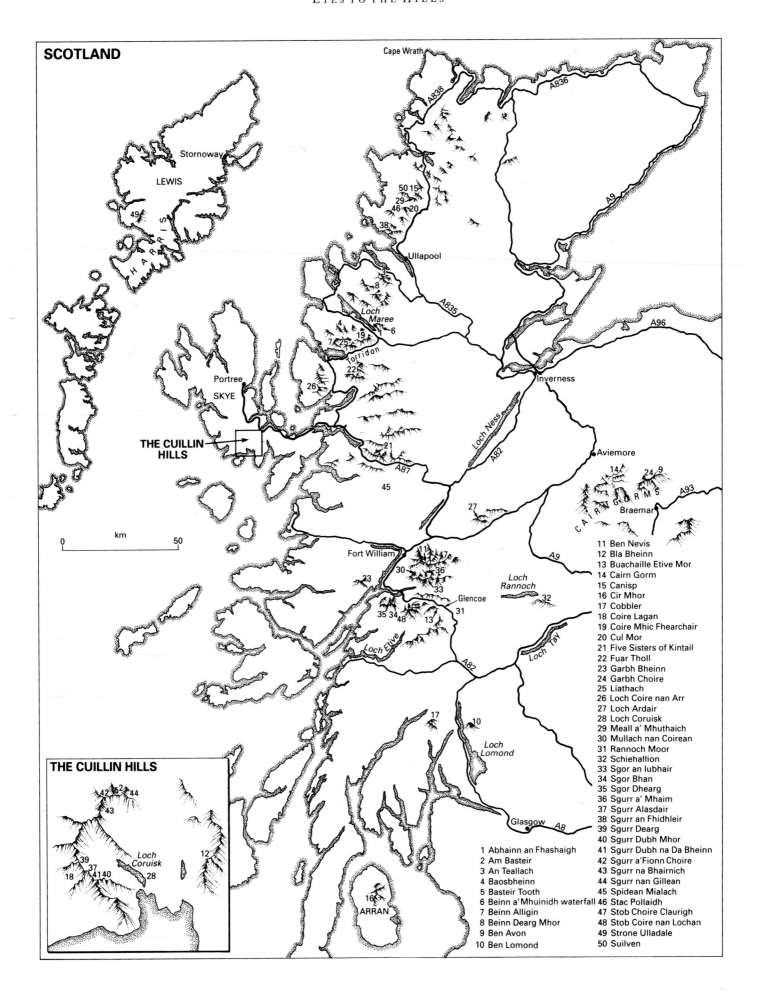

SCOTLAND

Cape Wrath

Stornoway

LEWIS

HARRIS

49

50 15
29
46 20

38

Ullapool

Loch
Maree

8

7 25
19
Torridon 6

22

Portree

SKYE

26

**THE CUILLIN
HILLS**

21

45

27

Inverness

Aviemore

14
24 9

CAIRNGORMS

Braemar

A93

A9

Fort William

11
47
30
36
33

23

Glencoe

35 34
48
13

31

Loch
Rannoch

32

Loch Etive

A82

Loch Tay

Loch Ness

A82

A87

A835

A838

A836

A9

A96

17

10

Loch
Lomond

Glasgow   A8

16
ARRAN

0   km   50

THE CUILLIN HILLS

42 2
43
44

39
37
18 4140

Loch
Coruisk

28

12

11 Ben Nevis
12 Bla Bheinn
13 Buachaille Etive Mor
14 Cairn Gorm
15 Canisp
16 Cir Mhor
17 Cobbler
18 Coire Lagan
19 Coire Mhic Fhearchair
20 Cul Mor
21 Five Sisters of Kintail
22 Fuar Tholl
23 Garbh Bheinn
24 Garbh Choire
25 Liathach
26 Loch Coire nan Arr
27 Loch Ardair
28 Loch Coruisk
29 Meall a' Mhuthaich
30 Mullach nan Coirean
31 Rannoch Moor
32 Schiehallion
33 Sgor an Iubhair
34 Sgor Bhan
35 Sgor Dhearg
36 Sgurr a' Mhaim
37 Sgurr Alasdair
38 Sgurr an Fhidhleir
39 Sgurr Dearg
40 Sgurr Dubh Mhor
41 Sgurr Dubh na Da Bheinn
42 Sgurr a'Fionn Choire
43 Sgurr na Bhairnich
44 Sgurr nan Gillean
45 Spidean Mialach
46 Stac Pollaidh
47 Stob Choire Claurigh
48 Stob Coire nan Lochan
49 Strone Ulladale
50 Suilven

1 Abhainn an Fhashaigh
2 Am Basteir
3 An Teallach
4 Baosbheinn
5 Basteir Tooth
6 Beinn a' Mhuinidh waterfall
7 Beinn Alligin
8 Beinn Dearg Mhor
9 Ben Avon
10 Ben Lomond

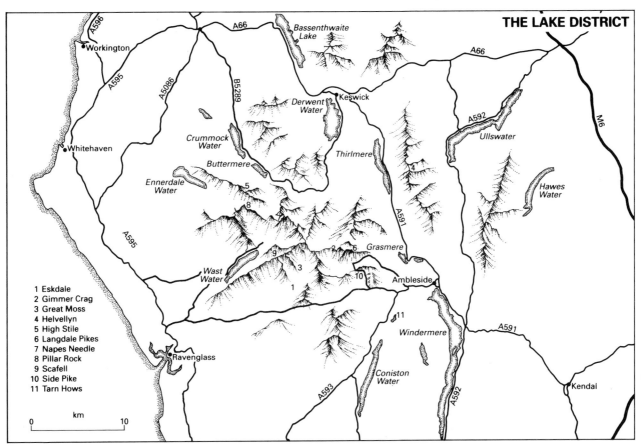

THE LAKE DISTRICT

1 Eskdale
2 Gimmer Crag
3 Great Moss
4 Helvellyn
5 High Stile
6 Langdale Pikes
7 Napes Needle
8 Pillar Rock
9 Scafell
10 Side Pike
11 Tarn Hows

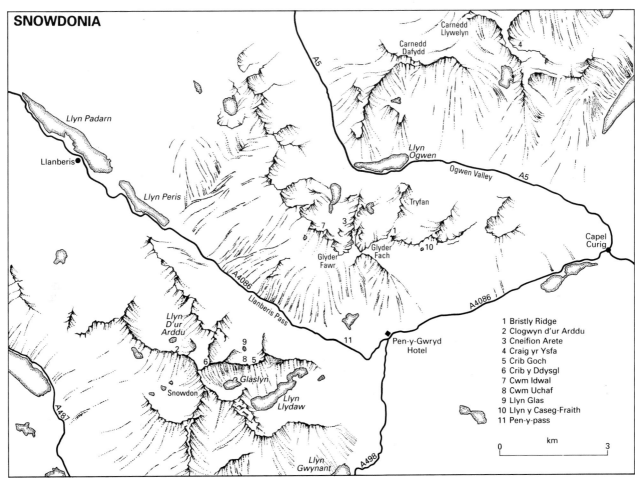

SNOWDONIA

1 Bristly Ridge
2 Clogwyn d'ur Arddu
3 Cneifion Arete
4 Craig yr Ysfa
5 Crib Goch
6 Crib y Ddysgl
7 Cwm Idwal
8 Cwm Uchaf
9 Llyn Glas
10 Llyn y Caseg-Fraith
11 Pen-y-pass

A NOTE ON THE PHOTOGRAPHY

All the photographs, except for five pictures in the text, were taken on medium ($2\frac{1}{4}''$ sq.) and large ($4'' \times 5''$) format cameras. Wherever possible a substantial tripod was employed but, even so, (as will be obvious from the relatively high shutter speeds used in many cases) wind was often a major problem. Indeed, bad weather was a serious obstacle from September 1989 until the end of March 1990. Fortunately this was followed by an exceptionally photogenic spring.

The vast majority of the photographs were taken over a 16-month period in 1989–90. Altogether 151 days were spent on location, of which 73 were 'under canvas'; many of the shots involved high camps or bivouacs on the mountain. All in all, 79 mountains were climbed, and a further uncounted number ascended part-way to reach a viewpoint. The camera gear was carried in a specially modified rucksack, which in winter weighed 18kgs, and on some high camping trips as much as 30kgs. At the end of it all I was fitter than I have ever been in my life, Alpine seasons included!

CAMERAS

Hasselblad 500 C/M 6×6 cm roll film SLR camera

MPP Mk7 $4'' \times 5''$ technical camera

Wista 45DX $4'' \times 5''$ field view camera (sometimes used with 6×9 cm roll film holder)

LENSES

FOR 4×5 CAMERAS:

90mm	Schneider Angulon 90mm F6.8
150mm	Schneider Apo Symmar-S 150mm F5.6
300mm	Rodenstock Apo-Ronar 300mm F9

FOR HASSELBLAD

50mm	Zeiss Distagon CF 50mm F4
80mm	Zeiss Planar CF 80mm F2.8
150mm	Zeiss Sonnar CF 150mm F4
TC	Teleplus MC6 $2 \times$ Teleconvertor

FILM STOCKS

EPR	Ektachrome 64 Professional 120
EPN	Ektachrome 100 Professional 120
EPP	Ektachrome 100 Plus Professional 120
PKR	Kodachrome 64 Professional 120
RFP	Fujichrome 50D Professional 120
RDP	Fujichrome 100D Professional 120
100RS	Agfachrome 100 RS Professional 120
6105	Ektachrome 100 Plus Professional 4×5 sheet film 6105
PC	Polaroid Professional Chrome 100 4×5 sheet film

FILTERS

SL	Skylight or 1A filter
UV	Ultraviolet filter
81A	81A filter
POL	Polarizer
GND	Graduated neutral density filter (1 stop)

Cover

MULLACH AN RATHAIN (1023m),
LIATHACH, FROM THE
NORTH-EAST
9.00 a.m. Late April

I left the road at 3.20 a.m. and walked in
darkness to this remote camera position to catch
the dawn. I had the camera all set up at 5.40
with time to spare – and to have a well-earned
cup of coffee. Although the dawn itself was
disappointing, it turned into an exceptionally
beautiful morning. I went into rhapsodies on my
pocket recorder: 'Idyllic up here. It doesn't look
like anything in Britain – it's more like
something in the Rockies' – then I got really
carried away '. . . or the Grandes Jorasses'.

Hasselblad   50mm   f16   1/30   POL   EPR

page 1

SUMMIT RIDGE OF SGURR A'
MHAIM (1099m)
4.30 p.m. Late April

Hasselblad   80mm   f13.5   1/250   SL   EPR

pages 2/3

THE MOUNTAINS OF ASSYNT AND
COIGACH FROM THE
NORTH-WEST
9.15 p.m. Late April

A geological 'unconformity', in which mountains
of Torridonian Sandstone are sitting on a
platform of much older Lewisian Gneiss, is
responsible for one of the most extraordinary
landscapes in Britain. Dr John MacCulloch
wrote in 1824 that the mountains looked 'as if
they had been shaken down at random out of a
pepper pot . . . having nothing to do with the
country or each other, either in shape, material,
position or character.' The peaks, from left to
right, are: Canisp (846m), Suilven (731m), Cul
Mor (849m), Cul Beag (769m), Stac Pollaidh
(613m), and Ben More Coigach (743m). None of
these outstanding mountains is a Munro.

MPP   90mm   f18   1/10   SL   6105

pages 4/5

BEINN ALLIGIN (985m) AND BEINN
DEARG (914m) FROM COIRE NA
CAIME
7.05 a.m. Late April

Hasselblad   80mm   f16   1/15   SL   EPR

pages 6/7

SGURR NAN GILLEAN AT DUSK
FROM SGURR BEAG, CUILLINS,
SKYE
10.40 p.m. Mid-June

Sgurr nan Gillean, 965m (the Peak of the Young
Men, or Gills), is arguably the finest and most
airy summit in Britain. It was first climbed by
the pioneer glaciologist and alpinist, Professor
James Forbes, in 1836. He was particularly
struck by the roughness of the gabbro; in fact he
said he had never seen rock 'so adapted for
clambering'. The route he took was the south-
east ridge (from where this picture was taken),
which later became known as the 'Tourist
Route', on account of the large number of
tourists who were taken this way to the summit
by guides in Victorian times. The Pinnacle Ridge
on the right, was climbed by the Pilkington
brothers of the Alpine Club in 1880. It remains
an ever-popular classic rock climb, graded
Difficult.

Hasselblad   80mm°   f4.7   1/60   SL   EPR

page 8

SHAFT OF LIGHT OVER SGURR NA
BHAIRNICH, CUILLIN RIDGE,
SKYE
7.00 p.m. Mid-June

This deep V-notch between the summits of An
Caisteal, 'The Castle', and Sgurr na Bhairnich

(pronounced VAIRnich), 'Peak of the Limpet', is the lowest point of the Cuillin Main Ridge, which never drops below 750m in 13km and, with some twenty tops of over 900m, is the finest mountain chain in the British Isles.

Hasselblad 150mm   f11 1/125 GND 100RS

page 12

TARN HOWS AND THE LANGDALE PIKES, CUMBRIA
2.00 p.m. Mid-November

Hasselblad 150mm   f8 1/125 81A EPR

left to right are: Sgurr an t-Searraich, Sgurr nan Saighead, Sgurr na Carnach and Sgurr na Ciste Duibhe. Far simpler just to call them the Five Sisters! The traverse of the whole ridge is a surprisingly arduous day.

Hasselblad 50mm   f16 1/60 UV EPR

page 9

AM BASTEIR LOOMS THROUGH THE MIST, CUILLIN RIDGE, SKYE
8.30 p.m. Mid-June

Taken from the West Ridge of Sgurr nan Gillean.

Hasselblad 150mm   f9.5 1/250 81A EPR

page 16

SGURR AN FHIDHLEIR (697m), COIGACH, NORTH-WEST SCOTLAND
12.00 a.m. Late April

The first ascent of this very imposing 300m high pyramidal buttress was not made until 1962, after many attempts since the turn of the century. One of the most compelling lines in the British Isles, it is said to be both sustained and serious for its grade (Very Severe).

Hasselblad 150mm   f5.6 1/250 POL EPR

page 14

LOCH CORUISK, SKYE
8.00 a.m. Mid-June

Hasselblad 80mm   f6.8 1/125 SL · EPR

page 10

COIRE TOLL AN LOCHAIN, AN TEALLACH
12.30 p.m. Late April

This 500m face – vaguely reminiscent of the Eigerwand in miniature – is one of the most impressive in the British Isles. The '1978 Face Route' traverses the top of the larger snowfield and then follows the obvious shallow gully line. I do not believe that it has been climbed very often.

Hasselblad 150mm   f4.7 1/250 81A EPR

page 15

THE FIVE SISTERS OF KINTAIL
6.10 p.m. Mid-April

The dominant snow-covered peak is Sgurr Fhuaran (1068m), while the other 'sisters' from

page 18

LIATHACH LOOMING ABOVE GLEN TORRIDON
2.30 p.m. Early April

Hasselblad 150mm   f8 1/500 81A EPR

page 19

BEINN ALLIGIN (985m) FROM THE
EAST AT DAWN
6.45 a.m. Late April

Beinn Alligin ('The Jewelled Mountain') is one
of the finest peaks of the Torridon area in
Wester Ross. It is however overshadowed in
every respect by its close neighbour Liathach.

Hasselblad   150mm + TC   f6.8   1/30   81A   EPR

page 20

CLOUD POURS OVER MEALL
CUMHANN, SEEN FROM BEN
NEVIS
7.45 a.m. Late March

In this view we are looking down quite steeply,
well over 300m.

Hasselblad   150mm   f11   1/250   81A   EPR

page 21

STRANGE CLOUDS OVER THE
DUBH RIDGE, CUILLINS, SKYE
5.30 a.m. Mid-June

I left our camp beside Loch Scavaig, itself a
remote spot, at 2.15 in the morning and walked
up to Druim Hain, one of the remotest places in
the Cuillins, to witness dawn on Sgurr nan
Gillean. Although this was a non-event, I was
compensated to some extent by what I
described on my dictaphone as 'quite
extraordinary things happening on the Dubh
Ridge.' The first ascent of this mountain, Sgurr
Dubh (pronounced DOO) in 1874 by the
legendary Alexander Nicolson, and his
subsequent descent of 900m in darkness has
been described rather extravagantly by B.H.
Humble as comparable with Whymper's first
ascent of the Matterhorn.

Hasselblad   150mm   f4   1/125   GND   EPR

page 22

AN TEALLACH (1062m), TOLL AN
LOCHAIN, AT DAWN
6.15 a.m. Late April

An Teallach ('The Forge') is regarded by many
hillwalkers and climbers – quite rightly, I think
– as the finest mountain in Britain. The
enormous (500m high) corrie facing us in this
picture, Toll an Lochain, with its great serrated
summit ridge – vaguely reminiscent of the

Trolltindene in Norway – has no equals in this
country. Amazingly the mountain was not
definitely climbed until 1893, up to which time it
had been cloaked in mystery and scarcely
featured on any map. Nowadays, and especially
in winter, it provides one of the great mountain
traverses of Britain.

Hasselblad   150mm   f5.6   1/60   81A   EPR

page 23

AN TEALLACH, TOLL AN
LOCHAIN, AFTER FRESH SNOW
6.45 a.m. Late April

The previous shot and this were taken on
consecutive days.

Hasselblad   150mm   f4.7   1/60   81A   EPR

page 24

MULLACH AN RATHAIN (1023m),
LIATHACH, FROM THE
NORTH-EAST
6.00 p.m. Early April

This picture was taken shortly after a heavy
blizzard.

Hasselblad   150mm   f6.8   1/500   81A   EPR

page 25

SUILVEN (731m) AFTER FRESH SNOW
6.50 a.m. Late April

To be sure of obtaining some interesting shots of Suilven (pronounced Soolven, meaning 'Pillar Mountain') I decided to camp below the east end of the mountain, some five miles from the road. No sooner had we got the tent up, than it started to snow – and carried on for three days, with very little respite. In fact, two nights running, at around 11 p.m., there was a bright thunderflash, and the storm wound itself up into a full-scale blizzard. From the photographic point of view this was obviously good news, for it transformed the landscape around us into a beautiful arctic wilderness. But life inside the minute two-man backpacking tent, without any reading matter (we had to resort to reading food wrappers), was not so amusing. We spent two and a half days flat on our backs – not unlike being in a two-man space capsule, I imagine – watching the snow hissing off the roof of the tent. The following was one of the high points in the conversation: 'This is bloody strange tasting coffee.' 'It's not coffee, it's tea.' The entry in my notebook for this shot, taken shortly after dawn on the fourth day, says simply: ' − 6°C, i.e. very cold!'

Hasselblad   150mm   f6.8   1/250   81A   EPR

page 26

BROCKEN SPECTRE NEAR THE SUMMIT OF BEN NEVIS
3.00 p.m. Mid-August

. . . Otherwise known as a self-portrait. This phenomenon, in which one's own shadow is projected into the mist and surrounded by a halo, is quite rare (I have seen it only three times in 25 years of climbing). It seems to require a very fine mist, and of course the sun has to be directly behind the observer and not too high in the sky. On this occasion it was so distinctive that I ran hysterically over to the summit cairn to draw other people's attention to it, but when we got back to the edge it had gone. 'I've got it on film,' I said lamely. But they didn't believe me.

Hasselblad   80mm   f11   1/125   SL   EPR

page 26

MYSTERIOUS CIRCLES ON BRANDON MOUNTAIN, SOUTH-WEST IRELAND
9.15 a.m. Late June

After a week of driving rain, I set off up Brandon Mountain in improving weather, and bivouacked under some boulders at about 300m. In the morning I walked up to the summit in thick cloud, then turned northwards towards the extraordinarily named subsidiary summit of 'Masatiompan'. About 1km north of the main summit (Grid ref: Q46 13, Sheet 20 Ordnance Survey of Ireland) I came across these strange circles in the grass on the very crest of the ridge. About 1½m in diameter (the rucksack in the photograph indicates the scale) and perfectly circular, they had all the appearance of well-worn animal tracks – though after a week of rain there was absolutely no sign of any footprints. It did not look like the work of any man-made implement, as the tracks were hard packed and worn, as if they had been formed over a considerable period of time. Nor was there any sign of any central pivot. None of the people I have shown this picture to have come up with a coherent explanation for such an extraordinary phenomenon in such a remote spot.

Pentax SP1000   55mm   f5.6   1/125   SL   KR

page 27

SUILVEN IN THE EVENING
7.10 p.m. Late April

Hasselblad   150mm   f13.5   1/250   81A   EPR

page 28

SUILVEN FROM LOCH MEALL A' MHUTHAICH ON A STORMY EVENING
7.15 p.m. Late April

Hasselblad   150mm   f11   1/250   81A   EPR

page 29

SUILVEN AT DAWN, AFTER A
STORM
6.15 a.m. Late April

Hasselblad   150mm   f4   1/125   81A   EPR

page 31

SUILVEN FROM THE EAST AT
DUSK
9.30 p.m. Late April

Hasselblad   80mm   f3.4   1/8   SL   EPR

page 34

THE NORTH FACE OF SGURR AN
FHIDHLEIR (697m), COIGACH
1.30 p.m. Late April

Hasselblad   150mm   f9.5   1/125   81A   EPR

page 30

TRIPLE BUTTRESS, COIRE MHIC
FHEARCHAIR, WESTER ROSS
7.20 p.m. Early April

Coire Mhic Fhearchair (pronounced
'Corryvikeraker') is undoubtedly one of the
finest corries in Britain. The stupendous
sandstone and quartzite 'Triple Buttress' – of
which the Central and the West can be seen
here – is nearly 300m high, and in a splendidly
remote position. It was first climbed by
Professor Normal Collie at the turn of the
century. The route he took was the gully
between these two buttresses, which were not
themselves climbed for another twenty years.
Recently the cliff has been the scene of some
very hard (Grade VI) winter climbs by, among
others, the climber cum tax-inspector
extraordinary from London, Mick Fowler.

Hasselblad   150mm   f9.5   1/60   81A   EPR

page 32

BEN LOMOND (974m) FROM THE
COBBLER AT DAWN
5.50 a.m. Mid-May

Hasselblad   150mm   f11   1/60   81A   RDP

page 35

TRYFAN (917m) FROM LLYN Y
CASEG-FRAITH
3.00 p.m. Late February

This was meant to be a winter shoot, but the
winter of 1989–90 was exceptionally mild (and
wet). Tryfan (which, incidentally, is correctly
pronounced 'Trurvan', and not the commonly
heard, anglicised 'Triffen' as in Triffid) is a
favourite mountain with many walkers and
climbers. Many rockclimbers have done their
first long easy climbs on the pleasant, sunny
East Face, seen here. It was quite rightly
described by the great pioneer George Abraham
as 'the mountain's chief glory'.

Hasselblad   80mm   f5.6   1/250   SL   EPR

pages 36/37

UPPER ESKDALE, FROM BORDER
END, CUMBRIA
1.30 p.m. Early November

My initial disappointment that Scafell was
completely hidden by cloud was very soon
compensated for by the superb lighting
conditions on this wild and windy day.

Hasselblad   50mm   f6.8   1/125   UV   EPR

page 38

QUARTZ PEBBLE ON FIACAILL A'
CHOIRE CHAIS, CAIRN GORM
(1245m)

Hasselblad   80mm   f4   1/60   SL   EPR

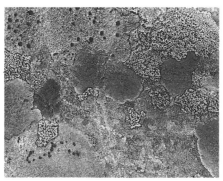

page 39

LICHEN ON BOULDER IN COIRE
ARDAIR, CENTRAL HIGHLANDS

Wista   150mm   f19   1/4   SL   PKR (6 × 9 back)

page 40

GRANULITE BOULDER IN LOCHAN
A' CHOIRE ARDAIR

Wista   150mm   f22   1/15   SL   6105

page 41

PEBBLES IN ALLT COIRE ARDAIR,
CENTRAL HIGHLANDS

Wista   150mm   f32   1/8   SL   PKR (6 × 9 back)

page 42

FOLDED MICA-SCHIST BELOW
THE NORTH PEAK OF THE
COBBLER

The folding of this late Pre-Cambrian mica-
schist occurred about four hundred million years
ago when it was raised above sea-level. The
vertical dimension shown in the photograph is
about 40cm (i.e. about three-quarters life size).

Hasselblad   80mm   f19   1/8   SL   RFP

page 43

LICHEN ON A BOULDER ON SRON
A' CHOIT, LOCH MAREE, WESTER
ROSS
4.50 p.m. Early November

Hasselblad   80mm   f6.8   8 secs   SL   EPN

page 44

COIRE LAGAN FROM THE SUMMIT
OF SGURR ALASDAIR, CUILLINS
6.30 p.m. Late June

Coire Lagan means 'Hollow Corrie', and
certainly as seen from the summit of Sgurr
Alasdair on the wild day I took this photograph
it resembled nothing so much as a giant, smoke-
filled cauldron. Sgurr Alasdair (Alexander's
Peak) is named after Alexander Nicolson who
made the first ascent in 1873. At 993m, it is the
highest mountain in the Cuillins and a fine
summit (but not as fine, I think, as Sgurr nan
Gillean).

Hasselblad   50mm   f8   1/60   SL   EPR

page 46

THE NORTH PEAK OF THE
COBBLER (884m) AT DAWN
6.15 a.m. Mid-May

The name, 'The Cobbler', is used of the whole
mountain and of the Centre Peak, while the
North Peak is, strictly speaking, the 'Cobbler's
Last'. This is another very young looking
mountain made of very ancient rock (570 million
year old Dalradian schist) – though its present
appearance is largely the result of the Ice Age,
which ended as 'recently' as ten thousand years
ago. It is without doubt one of the most
extraordinary mountains in the British Isles, and
yet it is ignored by the Munroists for no better
reason than that it fails to reach the height of

914m above sea level. Well, good: let them
leave it to climbers, and the lovers of amazing
rock sculpture. To get this shot I bivvied in the
open at this camera position on a very pleasant
grassy terrace directly below the North Peak.

Hasselblad   80mm   f8   1/30   SL   RDP

page 47

THE SUMMIT TOR OF BEN AVON
(1171m), CAIRNGORMS
1.30 p.m. Early June

Ben Avon (pronounced 'Ben Arn') means 'Fair
Mountain'. The summit tor is actually called
Leabaidh an Daimh Bhuidhe, which is
pronounced 'Lyeppy an Deff Vooya', and means
'The Couch of the Yellow Stag'. Just to
complicate things further, it is said that local
people do not call it this at all, as its real name
is Stob Dubh Easaidh Mor (pronounced 'Stope
Doo Essie More') – meaning 'The Black Point of
the Great Essie'. Which only leaves us with the
question, who or what is 'Essie'? A terrestrial
version of Nessie, perhaps?

Hasselblad   80mm   f4   1/125   SL   RFP

page 48

THE SKYLINE OF THE COBBLER
10.50 a.m. Mid-May

Hasselblad   80mm   f6.8   1/250   SL   RFP

pages 48/49

CLOUD POURS OVER THE CUILLIN
RIDGE, SKYE
10.00 p.m. Mid-June

Seen from the summit of Sgurr nan Gillean. The
summits in the distance, from left to right, are:
Sgurr Alasdair (993m), Sgurr Dearg (968m), and
Sgurr na Banachdich (965m).

Hasselblad   80mm   f4   1/125   SL   EPR

pages 50/51

AN TEALLACH (1062m), WESTER
ROSS, FROM THE EAST
7.15 a.m. Late April

Hasselblad   80mm   f19   1/30   SL   EPR

normal, the ridge is taken from south to north (that is, from right to left in the picture).

Hasselblad   150mm   f11   1/125   81A   EPR

page 52

THE BASTEIR TOOTH (916m) IN THE EVENING SUN
10.00 p.m. Mid-June

Note on my pocket recorder: 'Still boiling hot. Having great trouble keeping midges out of the camera when changing lenses or film. Plagued by them!'

Hasselblad   80mm   f4   1/125   SL   EPR

page 53

BASTEIR TOOTH FROM BELOW
4.45 p.m. Mid-June

Hasselblad   50mm   f9.5   1/125   UV   EPR

page 54

SCAFELL CRAG IN THE EVENING SUN
7.00 p.m. Early April

This is the finest crag in England and, being within a short distance of the highest point in the country, is the direct equivalent of Cloggy in Wales (see p.64). Even more than Cloggy though, it is steeped in history, as it has played a major role in British climbing from the very beginnings of the sport over a hundred years ago. On an evening like this, it is like a great Gothic cathedral, full of ghosts and memories.

Hasselblad   150mm   f6.8   1/125   81A   EPR

page 56

AM BASTEIR (936m) AND THE BASTEIR TOOTH, CUILLIN RIDGE, SKYE
8.45 a.m. Mid-June
Climber: Neil Drummond

Am Basteir (pronounced 'Am Barsiter') means 'The Executioner', probably because of the resemblance of the Tooth to a headsman's axe. Taken together they form what is undoubtedly one of the finest pieces of mountain sculpture in the British Isles. Of the two, the Tooth is considerably more difficult to climb, and forms one of the main obstacles in the traverse of the complete Cuillin Ridge – especially as it comes near the end of a very arduous day when, as is

page 57

BRISTLY RIDGE, GLYDER FACH (994m), SNOWDONIA, AT DUSK
5.15 p.m. Mid-February

Hasselblad   150mm   f5.6   1/30   81A   EPR

pages 58/59

'MITRE RIDGE', BEINN A' BHUIRD, CAIRNGORMS
6.00 p.m. Early June
Climbers: Alan Brown and Phil Sharkey

Garbh Choire (pronounced 'Garra Chorrie') on the north side of Beinn a' Bhuird (pronounced 'Ben a Voort') is one of the remotest crags in the country, involving a 15km approach walk into one of the great wildernesses of Western Europe. Large Format Photographers need to be very fit for this one! The climbers here are near the top of the classic 220m 'Mitre Ridge', which ends on this spectacular castellated crest.

Wista   300mm   f11   1/125   81A   6105

page 60

SUNRISE ON THE NORTH-EAST
BUTTRESS OF BEN NEVIS (1344m)
6.50 a.m. Late March

Known affectionately as 'the N.E.B.', this 600m
buttress is the finest and most powerful in
Britain – which is just as it should be, for it leads
directly to the highest point in the land. Both
the first ascent, by the remarkable
mathematician, scientist and inventor, Dr John
Hopkinson, with his son, Bernard, in 1892, and
the first winter ascent by W.W. Naismith and
party in April 1896 were notable for the
modesty of the pioneers. The 'Little Brenva
Face', to the left – so-called because of its alpine
character – was not exploited for its winter
climbing potential until the late 1950's. On this
particular morning it certainly looked extremely
alpine as the sunlight moved slowly down the
face.

Hasselblad   50mm   f6.8   1/125   SL   EPR

page 61

'DEVIL'S RIDGE' FROM SGURR A'
MHAIM
2.15 p.m. Late April

See also p.63.

Hasselblad   80mm   f13.5   1/250   SL   EPR

page 62

FIRST SNOW ON SPIDEAN
MIALACH (996m), KNOYDART, WEST
HIGHLANDS
1.15 p.m. Early November

The name of this mountain can be translated as
'The pinnacle of wild animals' or, less
attractively, as 'The peak of lice'. The
photograph was taken in very bad conditions
between heavy hail showers, which according to
my notes were 'almost continual after 11.00 a.m.
(poly bag over camera)'.

Hasselblad   150mm + TC f5.6   1/125 81A RDP

page 62

LONE CLIMBER ON THE NORTH-
EAST RIDGE OF SGOR BHAN (947m)
10.45 a.m. Mid-March

Sgor Bhan, the first peak of the Ballachulish
Horseshoe (Beinn a' Bheithir) – see also p.000 –
means 'White Peak', and is pronounced 'Skor
Varn'. The east-north-east ridge is a popular
Grade I/II winter climb.

Hasselblad   80mm   f11   1/125   SL   EPR

page 63

'DEVIL'S RIDGE' FROM THE
SUMMIT OF SGOR AN IUBHAIR
(1001m)
2.00 p.m. Late March

This knife-edged ridge, high above Fort William
(visible at the top of the picture), is part of the
excellent 'horseshoe' of peaks in the Mamores
that has become known as the 'Ring of Steall'.
The strange Gaelic name of the mountain from
which I took the photograph is pronounced Skor
an YOO-ir, and means Peak of the Yew.

Hasselblad   150mm   f9.5   1/250   81A   EPR

page 64

'WHITE SLAB', CLOGWYN D'UR
ARDDU, SNOWDON
8.00 p.m. Late July
Climbers: Johnny Dawes and Ros Townsend

White Slab (163m, E1) is one of the great classic
rock climbs of the British Isles. As Paul Williams
says in the climbing guidebook, 'an incredible
aura surrounds this fabled route; it exerts a
magic pull that compels one to climb it . . .
sooner, rather than later.' It is a perfect example
of a 'compelling line' that I talk about in
Chapter 4.

Wista   300mm   f11   1/30   81A   6105

page 65

SCAFELL PINNACLE, CUMBRIA
1.00 p.m. Mid-May

The climbers are on the ever-popular 'Slingsby's Route via Steep Ghyll', first climbed in 1888 by the great, larger-than-life Victorian climber, Cecil Slingsby, who was notable for his pioneering in Scotland and Norway as well as in the Lake District.

Hasselblad   800mm   f6.8   1/125   SL   RFP

page 66

DISTANT SGORR DHEARG (1024m)
FROM BEN NEVIS
8.00 a.m. Late March

Sgorr Dhearg (pronounced 'Skor Yerrak') means 'Red Peak'. It may look red in the summer, but in the winter it is a 'prodigious white fang', extremely enticing to the climber.

Hasselblad   150mm   f8   1/250   POL   EPR

page 67

ON THE SUMMIT RIDGE OF SGORR
DHEARG (1024m), ARGYLL
12.00 a.m. Mid-March
Climber: David Granger

Sgorr Dhearg is just one of the summits on the long and serpentine ridge west of Glencoe known as the 'Ballachulish Horseshoe' – more correctly called by its proper name, Beinn a' Bheithir, 'The Mountain of the Serpent'. In the 'Himalayan' conditions we found it on this day, with blue skies and spindrift flying, David Granger could hardly have wished for anything finer for his introduction to the Scottish mountains in winter.

Hasselblad   80mm   f13.5   1/125   SL   EPR

page 68

ON THE SUMMIT OF SCAFELL
PINNACLE
5.00 p.m. Mid-May
Climber: Colin Beechey

Descent is by a short climb or abseil down into Jordan Gap on the right, whence the main mountain is easily reached.

Hasselblad   80mm   f8   1/125   SL   RFP

page 69

SGURR NAN GILLEAN FROM THE
EAST AT DAWN
5.15 a.m. Mid-June

Hasselblad   150mm   f4   1/60   GND   EPR

page 70

SGURR FIONA (1059m), AN
TEALLACH, WESTER ROSS
12.45 p.m. Late April

Sgurr Fiona means 'Fair Peak', which is right, for it is certainly one of the finest in Britain – a fact which the Munroists took an extraordinarily long time to recognise. It was not until 1981 that they decided that this 'top' should be 'elevated to mountain status'.

Hasselblad   150mm   f19   1/60   81A   EPR

page 71

THE ORION FACE OF BEN NEVIS
5.30 p.m. Late March

There is nothing in Britain so sublime, in the full sense of the word, as the North Face of Ben Nevis in winter. And from the climbing point of view, there is nothing more serious. The climate is literally arctic and, like all great mountains, it should be left strictly alone in bad weather. On this particular day, using the 5 × 4 camera with a 300mm lens was extremely difficult as there was a strong, gusty wind and spindrift was flying everywhere. I had my full weight on the tripod a couple of times, and at one point I was afraid the bellows were going to be ripped clean off the camera. Fortunately, there were some sudden, unexpected lulls enabling me to take several shots. As this was the first day the face had been in condition for over two months there were many parties climbing, of which two are very clearly visible nearing the top of the Orion Face and Zero Gully.

| Wista | 300mm | f16 | 1/60 | 81A | 6105 |

page 72

ON SCAFELL PIKE, HIGH ABOVE
ESKDALE, CUMBRIA
8.45 a.m. Early April
Walker: Zbyszek Kotowicz

One of the first recorded explorations of this side of Scafell was by the poet, Samuel Taylor

Coleridge, in 1802. He was much given to wandering off the beaten track and venturing into the unknown. 'I *must* be alone if either my Imagination or Heart are to be enriched,' he insisted.

| Hasselblad | 150mm | f11 | 1/250 | 81A | EPR |

page 73

THE START OF THE MITRE RIDGE,
GARBH CHOIRE, CAIRNGORMS
3.30 p.m. Early June
Climber: Phil Sharkey

As the initial groove was streaming with water, Phil started up a variation just to its right. 220m to go! See also p.58.

| Hasselblad | 80mm | f9.5 | 1/125 | SL | PKR |

page 74

'MOSS LEDGE DIRECT', SCAFELL
PINNACLE
1.30 p.m. Mid-May
Climber: Colin Beechey

This very high quality 'Mild Very Severe' route was first climbed in 1925. Colin Beechey, seen here on the crux pitch, found it good but rather serious for its grade.

| Hasselblad | 80mm | f8 | 1/30 | SL | RFP |

page 75

STARTING THE CNEIFION ARETE,
SNOWDONIA
6.30 p.m. Early August
Climber: Gareth Fletcher

| Hasselblad | 80mm | f8 | 1/125 | SL | EPR |

page 75

'WEST FLANK ROUTE', CIR MHOR,
ISLE OF ARRAN
3.00 p.m. Early May
Climber: Robert Barton

The mountains of Arran have an extraordinarily remote feel for an island that is situated in the Firth of Clyde, only about 65km from the centre of Glasgow. This superb 150m 'Hard Very Severe' climb on perfect granite typifies the best of Arran climbing. Robert Barton is seen here at the top of the superlative crux pitch.

| Olympus XA 35mm | Ektachrome |

page 76

A STEEP SLAB ON THE CNEIFION
ARETE
7.15 p.m. Early August
Climber: Lisa White

Hasselblad   150mm   f6.8   1/250   81A   EPR

page 76

ON THE 'GREAT PITCH', THE
DEVIL'S KITCHEN, CWM IDWAL,
SNOWDONIA
4.30 p.m. Early August
Climber: Lisa White

The first ascent of this climb in 1898 by W.R.
Reade, was an extraordinarily bold
achievement. So outrageous was it considered
that George Abraham urged in his classic
guidebook ten years later that it 'be left severely
alone. Recent fatal accidents confirm that it is
not a justifiable climb by reason of the
peculiarly unreliable nature of the rock.'
Nowadays graded only 'V.Diff' it still has all the
atmosphere of a much more serious climb.
Although most of the loose rock has been
removed, in all but the driest weather it remains
unpleasantly slimy. To say it has 'character' is
an understatement.

Hasselblad   80mm   f2.8   1/60   SL   RDP

page 77

TRAVERSING OUT ON 'AURA',
AMPHITHEATRE WALL, CRAIG YR
YSFA, SNOWDONIA
1.45 p.m. Early August
Climber: Fred Hall

'Aura' – a tremendous 45m extreme (E2 5c)
pitch on perfect rock – is typical of many hard
mountain rock climbs in Britain that are situated
in awesome surroundings, far from the madding
crowd. Here this will always be true, for the
Amphitheatre Wall cannot be easily reached by
the ordinary walker. See also p.82.

Hasselblad   80mm   f6.8   1/125   SL   EPR

page 79

'JONES'S ROUTE DIRECT',
SCAFELL PINNACLE, CUMBRIA
4.00 p.m. Mid-May
Climber: Gavin Brown

This, one of the most famous classic rock climbs
in the Lake District, was first climbed by the
legendary Owen Glynne Jones in the 'vintage
year' of 1898. In concept, it was well ahead of
its time, and marked the end of the so-called
'Gully Era' (or, as one writer has put it, 'the
crossing of the evolutionary threshold from the
primordial slime to the dry land'). Gavin Brown
is seen here on the Mantelshelf, the traditional,
precarious crux, trying to get established on the
Toe Traverse. On his first attempt he tried to

climb it as a Hand Traverse, and fell off (about
3m). This was his second attempt, when he just
made it. The great O.G. ('Only Genuine') Jones
did not find it easy either: 'Standing on Walker's
shoulders I screwed myself out at the right-hand
top corner of our waiting-room . . . It was only
by pressing the body close to the wall, which
was fortunately a few degrees away from the
perpendicular, and by sliding the feet along
almost inch by inch, that the operation could be
effected.'

Hasselblad   80mm   f6.8   1/30   SL   RFP

page 80

THE FIRST PITCH OF 'THE GREAT
PROW', BLA BHEINN
1.30 p.m. Early July   Climber: Kerry Owen

Hasselblad   50mm   f4.7   1/30   GND on side   EPR

page 81

BEN MOON ON 'JERRY'S ROOF',
LLANBERIS PASS, SNOWDONIA
2.15 p.m. Mid-June

Most mortals would be unable to leave the
ground on this extreme boulder problem first
climbed by Jerry Moffatt in 1988.

Hasselblad   150mm   f8   1/30   81A   EPP

page 82

ON THE AMPHITHEATRE WALL,
CRAIG YR YSFA, SNOWDONIA
2.00 p.m. Early August
Climber: Fred Hall

Hasselblad   80mm   f6.8   1/125   SL   EPR

page 83

'GREAT SLAB', CLOGWYN D'UR
ARDDU, SNOWDON
3.45 p.m. Early August
Climbers: Andy Letchford and Julie Clover

Regarded at the time of its first ascent in June
1930, by Colin Kirkus and Graham MacPhee, as
'the boldest lead on British Rock', this 180m V.S.
has long been established as a mega-classic – a
truly 'Great' slab climb.

Hasselblad   80mm   f4   1/250   SL   EPR

page 84

LATE EVENING ON THE CNEIFION
ARETE ABOVE CWM IDWAL
8.45 p.m. Early August
Climber: Lisa White

Hasselblad   50mm   f4   1/60   UV   EPR

page 85

DAWN HEATWAVE ON THE
CUILLIN MAIN RIDGE, SKYE
5.30 a.m. Mid-June
Climber: Simon Ogsden

The climber in the photograph was doing the
complete traverse of the Main Ridge, and
bivvied a few hundred yards from myself the
other side of the ridge. Here he is returning
from collecting water from a spring which lies
only 90m below the summit of Sgurr a' Fionn
Choire. Unknown to him, I was following his
every movement with my camera set up on a
tripod on the main ridge above him. The first
complete traverse of the Main Ridge was made
in 1911 by L.G. Shadbolt and A.C. MacLaren in
12 hours 20 minutes from Gars Bheinn to Sgurr
nan Gillean. It has now been done in well under
four hours.

Hasselblad   150mm   f11   1/125   81A   EPR

page 87

'THE GREAT PROW', EAST FACE
OF BLA BHEINN, ISLE OF SKYE
5.45 p.m. Early July
Climber: Matt Andrews

This great 110m V.S. climb is probably most
notable for its splendid position 600m feet above
Loch Slapin. The price for this, however, is an
unusually long and arduous approach up very
steep scree.

Hasselblad   80mm   f11   1/125   SL   EPR

pages 88/89

'KIPLING GROOVE', GIMMER
CRAG, ABOVE LANGDALE,
CUMBRIA
4.15 p.m. Late May
Climber: Richard Hammond

Kipling Groove is the epitome of the classic
British mountain rock climb – a superb line, in a
beautiful setting, on perfect rock, with great
exposure and a committing crux just where it
should be – right near the top. It was first
climbed in 1948 by Arthur Dolphin who, apart
from being one of the best climbers of his day,
was a notable wit. He called it 'Kipling Groove'
because 'it's ruddy 'ard, mate!'

Wista   150mm   f16   1/60   SL   6105

page 90

MULLACH AN RATHAIN (1023m),
LIATHACH, FROM THE
NORTH-EAST
7.30 a.m. Late April

Note the avalanche fan which appeared
overnight.

| Hasselblad | 50mm | | f13.5 | 1/60 | GND | EPR |

page 92

GLENCOE, ARGYLL
10.15 a.m. Late March

This great valley, which is famous in the history
books for its bloody massacre of 1692, is
certainly one of the grandest in Britain. Thomas
Newte, passing through here in 1791, marvelled
at the most tremendous precipices he had 'ever
beheld in any part of the world'. Today it ranks
with Wasdale and Llanberis Pass for the classic
climbing it offers. A pity, then, that it should be
burdened with such uninspired mountain
names; for those seen here – Beinn Fhada,
Gearr Aonach, Aonach Dubh, and the
snowcapped Stob Coire nan Lochan behind –
mean nothing more exciting than Long
Mountain, Short Ridge, Black Ridge, and The
Peak . . . of the Corrie . . . of the Lochan.

| Wista | 90mm | | f22 | 1/25 | POL | 6105 |

pages 92/93

STOB COIRE NAN LOCHAN (1115m),
GLENCOE
11.00 a.m. Late March

| Wista | 300mm | | f19 | 1/30 | POL | 6105 |

page 94

ULLADALE RIVER, NORTH
HARRIS, OUTER HEBRIDES
4.15 p.m. Late September

This is a real wilderness, frequented only by a
few strange types with guns, fishing rods – or
climbing ropes. For here, overlooking the loch,
is Strone Ulladale, one of the most impressive
mountain crags in Britain (see p.116).

| Hasselblad | 150mm | | f9.5 | 1/125 | 81A | EPP |

page 95

OUTCROP NEAR HARD TARN,
RUTHWAITE COVE, GRISEDALE,
CUMBRIA
2.30 p.m. Late May
Rock: Borrowdale Volcanic Series

'A stone, when it is examined, will be found to
be a mountain in miniature. The fineness of
Nature's work is so great that, into a single
block, a foot or two in diameter, she can
compress as many changes of form and structure
on a small scale as she needs for her mountains
on a larger one' (John Ruskin, *Modern Painters*,
Vol. IV).

| Hasselblad | 150mm | | f19 | 1/30 | 81A | EPR |

page 95

PINNACLE WALL, CRAIG YR YSFA
4.45 p.m. Early August
Climbers: Fred Hall and Iwan Jones

The climb is 'Pinnaclissima' (E3).

| Hasselblad | 150mm | | f8 | 1/125 | 81A | EPR |

page 95

CUILLIN MAIN RIDGE FROM THE
SUMMIT OF SGURR DUBH NA DA
BHEINN
7.00 p.m. Early July

Sgurr Dubh na Da Bheinn (938m), pronounced
'Skoor Doo na Dah Ven', means simply, or
perhaps not so simply, 'The Black Peak of the
Two Mountains'. As it is a difficult name to
remember, I have long since fallen into the
habit of calling it, even more simply, 'Doo-dah'.
Whatever it's called, it is made of Peridotite, a
superb rough, light-coloured rock. Sgurr nan
Gillean and the Basteir Tooth are prominent in
the distance, at the northern end of the Cuillin
Ridge.

Hasselblad   50mm   f9.5   1/125   SL   EPR

page 97

SGURR A' FIONN CHOIRE AND AM
BASTEIR FROM SGURR NAN
GILLEAN
9.00 p.m. Mid-June

This was taken on June 21st (the longest day of
the year), and it was indeed a very long day.
The whole way up the West Ridge of Sgurr nan
Gillean – which in the beautiful evening light
above a sea of cloud was vaguely reminiscent of
something in the Alps – I had had amazing
retrospective views of Am Basteir looming
through the mist (see p.9), and now that I was
at the summit, it was still not letting me off the
hook, as I noted on my pocket recorder. I
added: 'It looks as if I'm going to be stuck up
here for a while.' I did not leave the summit
until 10.15 p.m.

Hasselblad   50mm   f9.5   1/125   UV   EPR

page 100

CRIB GOCH (921m) FROM BELOW
BWLCH COCH, SNOWDONIA
3.45 p.m. Late February

This classic pinnacled 'knife-edge' is the finest
section of the Snowdon Horseshoe (see pp.126,
162), which is one of the most popular ridge
walks in Britain.

Hasselblad   80mm   f8   1/15   SL   EPR

page 100

SNOWSTORM ON CRIB GOCH
5.00 p.m. Early March

On this particular day no one could have crossed
the ridge safely, as the wind was gusting up to
70 m.p.h.

Hasselblad   80mm   f8   1/30   SL   EPR

page 96

SGURR A' FIONN CHOIRE, BRUACH
NA FRITHE, AND AM BASTEIR
9.10 p.m. Mid-June

Sgurr a' Fionn Choire (935mm) – the peak of
the fair corrie; Bruach na Frithe (958m) – the
brae of the deer forest; and Am Basteir (936m)
– the Executioner. Seen from the summit of
Sgurr nan Gillean.

Hasselblad   150mm   f6.8   1/250   81A   EPR

page 99

BAOSBHEINN (875m), SHIELDAIG
FOREST, WESTER ROSS
12.15 p.m. Early November

Poor old Baosbheinn, 'The Wizard's Mountain'
– it's miles from anywhere and not even a
Munro, and yet it has a magic and mystery all of
its own. Of what possible relevance to it are
rational numbers and the world of man?

Hasselblad   150mm   f8   1/250   81A   EPP

page 101

CRIB GOCH AND LLYN GLAS
AFTER FRESH SNOW
3.40 p.m. Early March

Hasselblad   80mm   f16   1/30   SL   EPR

pages 102/103

RANNOCH MOOR AFTER A
SNOWSTORM
2.00 p.m. Late March

MPP   90mm   f32   1/50   No filter   PC

page 104

LOCH COIRE NAN ARR,
APPLECROSS, WESTER ROSS
10.00 a.m. Late September

This photograph was taken from the tent on one

of my many autumn trips that was frustrated by bad weather. This particular camp, 'only' a mile and a half from the road, was memorable for a trip back from the Applecross Hotel late one night, when Andrew Robson and I got hopelessly lost (and very wet) crossing innumerable streams and bogs, and were quite unable to find the tent, despite an extensive search with our head torches. We were just on the point of giving up and returning the whole horrible boggy way back to the car when one of the many tent-shaped boulders we encountered decided to transmute itself into our tent as we approached. On such a night a four-star hotel could not have been more welcome.

Hasselblad   80mm   f13.5   1/250   SL   EPP

page 105

STREAM ON THE SOUTH FLANK OF
FUAR THOLL (907m), WESTER ROSS
6.30 p.m. Late September

One of the consolations of days of bad weather in the mountains is that it at least brings out all the richness of the moss and lichen, so that useful close-up work can still be done. This was taken at a height of about 500m on the west side of a vast area of overlapping slabs above the shoulder of Sgurr a' Mhuilinn.

Hasselblad   80mm   f13.5   1 sec   SL   EPR

page 106

BEINN A' MHUINIDH WATERFALL,
WESTER ROSS
3.00 p.m. Early November

Beinn a' Mhuinidh (pronounced 'Ben a Voony') is named rather crudely after its prominent 90m waterfall, for it means the 'Mountain of Urinating'. In keeping with this watery theme, it was also urinating with rain (to put it politely) when I took this picture. A remarkable rock climb was made up the face to the left of the waterfall in 1899 by G.T. Glover and Dr W. Inglis Clarke, who agreed that 'the beautiful, both in rock scenery and hand and footholds, had been sought and found'.

Hasselblad   80mm   f3.5   1/60   SL   EPN

page 107

ROWAN TREE BESIDE ABHAINN AN
FHASHAIGH, WESTER ROSS
5.15 p.m. Late October

The beautiful sounding name of this river (pronounced Avin an Ahssy) sadly does not mean anything more exciting than 'River of the Dwelling'. It was raining hard when I took this picture and my tone of voice on my pocket recorder was distinctly jaded: 'Very difficult conditions after 24 hours on the hill.' I had in fact bivvied out in an extremely remote spot several miles to the north in the hope of a fine dawn which never materialised. Perhaps my mood would have improved if I had eaten some of the rowan tree berries, which are said to have magical properties and are used in herbal remedies.

Hasselblad   80mm   f9.5   1 sec   SL   EPN

page 108

BUTTERMERE IN THE AUTUMN
11 a.m. Late October

This is arguably the most beautiful of all the Lakeland valleys. Wonderfully deserted off-season, it becomes – like everywhere else in the Lake District – completely swamped by tourists at the height of the summer and at Bank Holidays.

Hasselblad   50mm   f9.5   1/125   UV   EPR

page 110

MULLACH NAN COIREAN (939m) FROM SGURR A' MHAIM
2.30 p.m. Late April

Mullach nan Coirean means, very appropriately, 'The summit of the corries'. The faces seen here are about 500m high.

Hasselblad   150mm   f9.5   1/500   81A   EPR

page 111

CWM UCHAF AND LLYN GLAS AT DUSK, SNOWDONIA
6.15 p.m. Early March

From this viewpoint we are looking out over Llanberis towards Anglesey. Shortly after I took this picture a blizzard started, making it extremely difficult to see what I was doing, as I walked straight into the driving snow with the head torch on. I made no attempt to find the proper route but just headed straight down steep slopes with my crampons on into Cwm Glas. Almost as soon as I reached safe ground the snow stopped and the stars came out. But it was extremely cold, and the road down Llanberis Pass was already very icy.

Hasselblad   80mm   f4   1/4   SL   EPR

pages 112/113

LIATHACH (1054m) FROM BEN EIGHE, TORRIDON, WESTER ROSS
10.15 a.m. Early April

Most hillwalkers and climbers will put Liathach ('The Grey One') high in their list of the 'top ten' mountains of Britain. Despite the exceptional age of its rock (around 1,000 million years), it has an extraordinarily rough-hewn, unfinished appearance. The main summit, Spidean a' Choire Leith, is like a crude and massive fortress, that is topped in the winter by the most elegant of snow ridges. There is some confusion over the pronunciation of the name:

most climbers call it 'Lia-tar', those 'in the know' pronounce it 'Lia-gar', while the locals simply call it 'Lia-ha' – which is good enough for me.

Wista   300mm   f19   1/125   81A   PKR (6 × 9 back)

page 114

CORRAG BHUIDHE PINNACLES (1044m), AN TEALLACH, WESTER ROSS
1.00 p.m. Late April

Hasselblad   150mm   f11   1/125   81A   EPR

page 115

'THE APPIAN WAY', PILLAR ROCK, CUMBRIA
4.15 p.m. Late August
Climbers: Simon Robinson and Nick Blunt

The west face of Pillar Rock is in a wonderfully remote position – in the context of the Lake District – high above the lonely valley of Ennerdale. Here one can enjoy climbs with a very traditional flavour, for if climbing in Britain started anywhere it was on this great isolated rock bastion. As an elderly farmer said to H.M. Kelly (who made the first ascent of 'the Appian Way', the Hard Severe climb shown here): 'Ay, it's a grand stone.'

Hasselblad   150mm   f6.8   1/125   81A   RDP

page 116

pages 118/119

pages 122/123

A NEW CLIMB ON STRONE
ULLADALE, NORTH HARRIS,
OUTER HEBRIDES
6.30 p.m. Late September
Climber: Ben Moon

A WILD EVENING IN COIRE MHIC
FHEARCHAIR, TORRIDON
7.30 p.m. Early April

BUACHAILLE ETIVE MOR (1022m) AT
SUNRISE
7.30 a.m. Late March

Everything about Strone Ulladale is superlative:
the oldest rock, the remotest crag, the biggest
overhang (45m in 150m), the hardest routes, the
worst weather, the strongest winds, and last but
not least – when the wind drops – the most
voracious midges. If you have left your Moskil
(an anti-midge smoke coil) behind, you might as
well take the first ferry back to the mainland.
Any climber who claims to have been to Strone
but does not know the meaning of the word
'Moskil' is a liar. The crag is made of Lewisian
gneiss, the oldest rock of the Continental Shield
(almost 3,000 million years old), and, looking up
at those overhangs, there is indeed a curious
sense of being under the edge of the earth's
crust, face to face with the most basic material
in the world. Unfortunately our arrival
coincided with that of Hurricane Gabrielle, and
this was the only fine day we had. The climbing
team (undoubtedly the strongest ever assembled
here) – of Johnny Dawes, Paul Pritchard, and
Ben Moon – quickly went to work on their new
line. By late evening they had worked out the
difficult entry through the initial overhangs and
Ben Moon raced up the long, overhung slab-
ramp above to take a hanging belay. At which
point the last rays of the sun very obligingly
struck the edge of the face. In failing light
Johnny forged on up the overhanging crack
above. Next day they were just able to complete
the climb (Grade E6, 6b) before the onset of
Hurricane Hugo. Johnny asked me if I had any
ideas for a route name, and I said that in a
curious way it reminded me of 'Moss Ghyll
Grooves' on Scafell – tipped forward through 30
degrees! It would be nice if we could think of a
pun on Moss Ghyll Grooves as a sort of tribute
to that much easier climb. Johnny looked at me
as if I must be mad. 'Moskil Grooves,' he said.

Hasselblad 150mm+TC f4.7 1/60 81A EPP

My notes here are full of drama: 'Working very
fast indeed, in serious conditions, five miles from
the road, on own, in blizzard'. I do remember
that, as well as various other appendages, the
dial on my light meter froze up completely.
Montage of 2 shots, each:

Hasselblad 150mm f6.8 1/125 81A EPR

page 120

SIDE PIKE, LANGDALE, CUMBRIA
12 a.m. Early November

The mountains behind are Harrison Stickle
(736m), and Pavey Ark (723m).

Hasselblad 150mm f4.7 1/250 SL EPR

'The Great Herdsman of Etive' (pronounced
roughly, 'Bookle Etiv Mor') is a Muhammed Ali
among mountains. Standing arrogantly at the
western end of Rannoch Moor, it says simply 'I
am the greatest'. It has occupied a major
position in British rock and ice climbing
throughout the history of the sport. The snow
gully running down just left of the summit was
first climbed by the legendary Harold Raeburn
in 1909, while the deep slot just right of the
summit, Raven's Gully, was climbed by Hamish
MacInnes and a youthful Chris Bonington in
1953. Both were major achievements in their
day. In summer, the buttresses provide
superlative, exposed rock climbs of all standards.

Wista 150mm f19 1/8 SL PC

page 124

IMPROVING WEATHER OVER
LLANBERIS PASS
9.00 p.m. Late July

Hasselblad 150mm f5.6 1/125 81A RDP

pages 124/125

SNOWDON (1085m) EMERGES FROM
THE CLOUDS
10.15 a.m. Early April

I had been in this camera position for four hours
before the cloud started to lift. My notes say
simply, 'Most nerve-wracking shoot I've ever
done.'

Wista   150mm   f27   1/60   SL   6105

pages 126/127

CRIB GOCH (923m), SNOWDON (1085m),
AND CRIB Y DDYSGL (1065m)
11.00 a.m. Early April

The ridge from Crib Goch to Crib y Ddysgl
(pronounced Crib-a-Thisgul) is the finest section
of the Snowdon Horseshoe.

Wista   150mm   f16   1/30   POL   6105

page 128

RAIN SWEEPING UP LOCH MAREE,
WESTER ROSS
3.00 p.m. Early November

Loch Maree, hemmed in by ancient mountains
and forests, has with justification been called
the finest inland lake in the country. It was
named after the Celtic Saint Maelrubha, who
ruled as an abbot here in the 7th Century. The
beautiful and mysterious islands are still
forested with ancient Caledonian pines, said to
be thousands of years old. One of them, the
'Holy Isle Maree', is famous for rites involving
the sacrifice of bulls to Saint Maelrubha, which
were carried out well into the seventeenth
century. More recently it was visited by Queen
Victoria, who stuck coins into a sacred tree.
There is also a well which is supposed to cure
insanity, and in Victorian times this was still
being used, occasionally with success. On this
particular trip I was nearly driven insane myself
by the appalling weather: on the day I took this
picture my notes say simply, 'Like yesterday,
but worse. Almost continuous showers.'

Hasselblad   50mm   f4   1/60   UV   RDP

page 129

RAINBOW OVER LOCH MAREE,
WESTER ROSS
1.00 p.m. Early November

Hasselblad   150mm   f6.8   1/250   81A   RDP

page 130

CUL MOR (849m), ASSYNT, NORTH-
WEST SCOTLAND
8.15 p.m. Late April

After we had been marooned for three days in
our tent by a blizzard, the weather cleared so
we attempted to climb Suilven. As the gale had
been coming from the north, I decided to tackle
the mountain from the south, in the mistaken
belief that there would be less snow to contend
with on that side. Before long we found
ourselves floundering waist-deep in powder
snow and, as we were fast running out of
daylight, we gave up. As a consolation we were
rewarded with this superb sunset view of the
empty wilderness of the Inverpolly Nature
Reserve. We had to return to our tent amongst
the maze of lochans east of Suilven on compass
bearings, in the dark.

Hasselblad   80mm   f4.7   1/125   SL   EPR

page 131

LOCH HARPORT AT DUSK, FROM
CUILLIN MAIN RIDGE, SKYE
11.30 p.m. Mid-June

The most beautiful night I have ever spent in
the British mountains was on a superb mossy
ledge on the main ridge of the Cuillins just
below the summit of Sgurr a' Fionn Choire
(935m) – 'The Peak of the Fair Corrie'. I had a
bivvy bag, but no sleeping bag, as it was very

warm. Actually, it was a very short night, as I had to be up again at 4.30 a.m. to photograph the dawn (see p.132).

Hasselblad   150mm   f5.6   1/2   81A   100RS

page 132

SUNRISE BEHIND THE BASTEIR TOOTH (916m), SKYE
5.10 a.m. Mid-June

The hill on the left in the mid-distance is in fact Glamaig, which I am rather rude about in the text (p.146).

Hasselblad   80mm   f22   1/60   SL   EPR

page 133

'THE GREAT PROW' OF BLA BHEINN CATCHES THE EVENING LIGHT
9.10 p.m. Early July

After a long photo session on the summit of Bla Bheinn (928m) – pronounced 'Blarven' – I set off down in fading light. With no prospect of any more interesting photography I put the camera away, but as usual I had one frame left for the unexpected – which was just as well, for as I neared the Great Prow, which I had been taking pictures of earlier in the day (p.87), its crest was suddenly aflame with the last rays of the sun. It only lasted for a few seconds, and then it was

gone. And with that last frame taken, so was I. It was in fact the last picture of the trip, for the next day I had to be back in London.

Hasselblad   150mm   f4   1/250   81A   EPR

page 134

THE NORTH-EAST BUTTRESS OF BEN NEVIS
7.50 a.m. Late March

(See also pp.60, 71.)

Hasselblad   50mm   f11   1/125   POL   EPR

pages 134/135

SCHIEHALLION (1083m) SEEN FROM BEN NEVIS AT DAWN
7.30 a.m. Late March

This was a supreme case of suddenly finding my looking at a dream image which had become something of an obsession: a temperature inversion from Ben Nevis in winter. It was also a classic case of going up to a high camp (outside the CIC Hut) in bad weather to catch a 'window' in the weather that was forecast for dawn. When we left our tent at 6.00 a.m. the top of Ben Nevis was still in the mist. Dave Granger and I both gasped at the beauty of the scene which confronted us when we stepped onto the Carn Mor Dearg Arete at the head of Coire Leis. There followed a frenetic half hour

of photography at −7°C. We then continued up the ridge to the summit of Britain, and on this particular morning, high above that ocean of cloud, it seemed like a stairway to heaven. We met one other person, descending from the summit, and given that the whole spectacle only lasted about an hour and a half, we felt very privileged indeed.

Hasselblad   150mm   f11   1/250   SL   EPR

pages 136/137

THE MAMORES FROM BEN NEVIS AT DAWN
8.00 a.m. Late March

The summits from left to right are: Stob Coire a' Chairn (981m), Am Bodach – 'The Old Man' (1032m), and Sgurr a' Mhaim (pronounced 'Skoor a Vaim') – 'The Peak of the Breast' (1099m). These peaks are taken in by an excellent mountain day called 'The Ring of Steall' which starts and finishes at Steall Cottage in Glen Nevis. (See also pp.61, 153).
Montage of 2 shots, each:

Hasselblad   150mm   f8   1/250   POL   EPR

page 138

CAIRN ON THE EAST RIDGE OF SCHIEHALLION, GRAMPIANS
5.30 p.m. Early August

The mystique of Schiehallion (1083m), which

apparently means 'The Fairy Hill of the Caledonians' (though I am not quite sure how the Caledonians get into it), is all the greater for its associations with a famous experiment carried out by the Astronomer Royal in 1774 to measure the mass of the earth. He chose Schiehallion because of its unusually conical cross-section (see p.135). His results have been shown by modern instruments to be extraordinarily accurate. It was while he was engaged on this task that one of the survey team, Charles Hutton, dreamt up the idea of using contour lines in mapping.

Hasselblad   80mm   f9.5   1/125   SL   EPR

page 140

SUNSET FROM SRON NA CICHE, ISLE OF SKYE
10.15 p.m. Early July

In this view we are looking out over the westernmost point of the Isle of Skye, known as Duirinish, towards the distant Outer Hebrides.

Hasselblad   150mm   f8   1/60   No filter   EPR

page 141

TRYFAN AT SUNRISE
6.30 a.m. Early April

Hasselblad   150mm+TC   f9.5   1/4   81A   RFP

pages 142/143

LOOKING UP LOCH ETIVE TOWARDS GLENCOE, EVENING
8.35 p.m. Late May

Wista   150mm   f19   1/8   POL+GND   6105

pages 144/145

THE SAME, AT DUSK
9.30 p.m. Late May

Wista   150mm   f16   1/8   GND   6105

page 146

SGURR NAN GILLEAN FROM THE WEST
5.45 p.m. Late June

Hasselblad   150mm   f6.8   1/250   81A   EPR

page 147

STREAM ON THE SOUTH FLANK OF FUAR THOLL (907m), WESTER ROSS
6.45 p.m. Late September

Hasselblad   80mm   f22   2 secs   SL   EPR

page 148

GARBH BHEINN (885m), ARDGOUR, WESTERN HIGHLANDS
1.00 p.m. Late March

Pronounced 'Garraven', meaning Rough Mountain. If ever there was a mountain that makes a complete nonsense of the concept of 'Munros', it is this mighty fortress of superb gneiss (pronounced 'nice', which it is – very). Here there are some superb rock climbs, and good ice climbs in a hard winter.

Hasselblad   150mm   f4.7   1/500   81A   EPR

page 149

COIRE LAGAN, CUILLINS, SKYE –
EVENING
8.45 p.m. Late June

Hasselblad   80mm   f5.6   1/60   SL   EPR

pages 150/151

STRIDING EDGE, HELVELLYN
(950m), CUMBRIA
12.30 p.m. Late May

Montage of two frames, each:

Hasselblad 150mm + TC f5.6 1/125 GND EPN

page 151

'BELLE VUE BASTION', EAST FACE
OF TRYFAN, SNOWDONIA
2.00 p.m. Late July
Climbers: Nick Gregory and Rosamund Bell

Long before its first ascent by Ivan Waller in
1927 this superbly situated buttress high above
the Ogwen Valley was regarded as an obvious
challenge. Before he led it, Waller climbed it
with a top rope for protection, but soon
afterwards he repeated it solo (i.e. with no rope
at all). Nick Gregory is seen here on the second
main pitch, having just traversed out onto the
nose from the 'Grove of Bollards'. The pitch
ends abruptly at the clean-cut 'Belle Vue
Terrace', on which, legend has it, Ivan Waller
had a gramophone playing when he made the
first ascent.

Hasselblad   150mm   f6.8   1/125   81A   RDP

page 152

LOOKING DOWN ON ENNERDALE
FROM GREY CRAG, HIGH STILE,
CUMBRIA
3.30 p.m. Late May

Hasselblad   80mm   f4   1/125   SL   EPR

page 153

TWO WALKERS ON SGURR A'
MHAIM IN THE MAMORES
2.30 p.m. Late April
Walkers: George Graham and Jan Scott

The mountain behind is Am Bodach (1032m),
'The Old Man'. (See also p.136.)

Hasselblad   80mm   f9.5   1/250   SL   EPR

page 154

THE 'ZIG-ZAGS' AT THE TOP OF
THE PIG TRACK, SNOWDON
2.30 p.m. Early August

The 'Pig Track' is so called because it crosses,
en route, Bwlch y Moch, 'The col of the pigs'.
However, many clever types over the years
have assumed that it is the PYG track, short for
Pen y Gwryd – even though it does not start
anywhere near the Pen y Gwryd hotel.

Hasselblad   50mm   f4.7   1/60   UV   EPR

page 155

ABSEILING DOWN THE
INACCESSIBLE PINNACLE, SGURR
DEARG, CUILLINS
7.15 p.m. Late June
Climber: Nick McEvett

The mountain Nick McEvett is looking at is
Sgurr Alasdair, the highest in the Cuillins (see
also p.44). The prominent 'Great Stone Shoot'
on its left side, which used to be one of the best
scree runs in Britain, has now been largely
destroyed by over-use.

Hasselblad   50mm   f8   1/125   UV   EPR

page 157

WALKERS BESIDE GREAT MOSS,
UPPER ESKDALE, CUMBRIA
1.30 p.m. Late March

The Great Moss of Upper Eskdale can also be
seen, from completely different viewpoints, on
pp.37, 72.

Hasselblad   50mm   f8   1/125   UV   EPR

page 160

MORNING ON MEALL A'
MHUTHAICH, ASSYNT, AFTER A
SNOWSTORM
6.40 a.m. Late April

The mountain behind is Cul Mor (849m) – see
also p.130.

Hasselblad   50mm   f9.5   1/30   UV   EPR

page 156

NORMAN CROUCHER STARTING
UP CRIB GOCH, SNOWDONIA
11.30 a.m. Late July

Since losing both legs in a railway accident at
the age of 18, Norman Croucher has achieved
an extraordinary catalogue of ascents
throughout the world on his artificial legs.
Although he never needs crutches for ordinary
walking, he normally uses them on rough
mountain ground for added stability, as seen
here on the relatively tame mountains of North
Wales. By adding spikes, he can also use them
on snow and ice up to 40°; and on Muztagh Ata
in China he used them practically the whole
way to the summit at 7,548m   35mm

page 158

BEINN DEARG MHOR, WESTER
ROSS, FROM THE EAST
7.00 a.m. Late April

Attaining the height of 'only' 908m, this is
another mountain which makes a nonsense of
the concept of 'Munros'. As I saw it on this
particular morning, reflected in an unnamed
lochan in the utter desolation of the 'Dundonnel
Forest' I was overwhelmed by its serene
grandeur. It is pronounced, incidentally, 'Ben
Jerak Voar'.

Hasselblad   150mm   f6.8   1/125   81A   EPR

page 161

STAC POLLAIDH (613m) FROM THE
NORTH AT DUSK
9.30 p.m. Late April

Hasselblad   80mm   f3.4   1 sec   SL   EPR

page 162

NORMAN CROUCHER TRAVERSING
CRIB GOCH
1.00 p.m. Late July

The crutches no longer of any use to him on the
narrow summit ridge, Norman strapped them to
his rucksack and traversed the airy crest with an
ease that would have put many an able-bodied
climber to shame.   35mm

page 163

NAPES NEEDLE, ABOVE WASDALE,
CUMBRIA
1.00 p.m. Late August
Climber: Unknown

The solo first ascent of Napes Needle by W.P.
Haskett Smith in 1886 is often – rather
arbitrarily – regarded as the 'birth of British
rockclimbing', for it was pre-dated by the
Inaccessible Pinnacle, 1880 (p.166), Scafell
Pinnacle, 1884 (p.68), and two major routes on
the West Buttress of Lliwedd in 1883 and 1884.
All these were serious undertakings demanding
the use of a rope and no small amount of
technique. Napes Needle was, however,
unquestionably a full grade harder (V.Diff) than
anything that had ever been climbed before.
Haskett Smith had in fact spent four previous
summers in Wasdale before he attempted the
Needle; and it was he indeed who made the
first ascent of Scafell Pinnacle, both from the
Jordan Gap and from the much longer Steep
Ghyll side, in 1884. At the foot of Napes Needle,
he threw up some stones to test the flatness of

the summit. 'Out of three missiles one consented
to stay, and thereby encouraged me to start,
feeling as small as a mouse climbing a
milestone.' And a milestone it certainly was.

Hasselblad   50mm   f11   1/125   UV   EPN

page 164

OUTSIDE EDGE ROUTE, CRAIG YR
OGOF, CWM SILYN
1.00 p.m. Early August
Climber: David Rothering

This 120m V. Diff is one of the best climbs of its
standard in North Wales. It was first climbed in
July 1931 by J. Menlove Edwards.

Hasselblad   150mm   f6.8   1/250   81A   EPR

page 165

NORMAN CROUCHER ON CRIB
GOCH (921m)
1.30 p.m. Late July   35mm

page 166

INACCESSIBLE PINNACLE (986m),
SGURR DEARG, CUILLINS, SKYE
7.00 p.m. Late June
Climbers: Marisa Damaso, Mike Romaniuk,
Nick McEvett and Rick Garbutt

The 'Inaccessible Pinnacle' remains the most
inaccessible major mountain summit in Britain.
There is no way one can walk past it and claim
(as some do) that one has climbed Sgurr Dearg,
the second highest mountain in the Cuillins. The
first ascent of the pinnacle by the East Ridge (on
the far side in the photograph) in August 1880
by Lawrence and Charles Pilkington, after
several seasons' experience in the Alps, was a
major historical achievement, pre-dating that of
Napes Needle (p.163) by six years. Here, as is
common, a party are descending by abseil down
the shorter, west side.

Hasselblad   50mm   f9.5   1/125   UV   EPR

page 167

HIGH SPIRITS ON SCAFELL PIKE
(978m)
9.00 a.m. Early April
Walker: Zbyszek Kotowicz

Hasselblad   150mm   f11   1/250   81A   EPR

page 167

BEN MOON AND JOHNNY DAWES
AFTER THE FIRST ASCENT OF
'MOSS KILL GROOVES', STRONE
ULLADALE
12.00 a.m. Late September

Hasselblad   80mm   f2.8   1/30   SL   EPP

pages 170/171

CRIB GOCH, SNOWDON AND CRIB
Y DDYSGL FROM THE NORTH-EAST
11.30 a.m. Early April

I had been in this camera position for over 5
hours, and soon it would be time to descend.

Wista   300mm   f27   1/60   81A   6105

pages 168/169

ACROSS THE 'GREY CORRIES' TO
BEN NEVIS, FROM STOB CHOIRE
CLAURIGH
12.15 p.m. Late April

This has to be a contender for one of the finest
mountain views in Britain. Fortunately it will
never become a tourist attraction because Stob
Choire Claurigh (1177m – 'meaning obscure') is
only within the range of the fit and dedicated
mountain walker. There is nothing at all grey or
obscure about the so-called 'Grey Corries' in
winter, when they are transformed into a white
wilderness of exceptional beauty.

Wista   300mm   f16   1/250   SL   6105

page 172

PEN Y PASS, SNOWDONIA, AT
SUNSET
9.15 p.m. Late July

Pen y Pass, known to thousands of walkers as
one of the main starting points for Snowdon,
has, like Wasdale Head in the Lake District, a
climbing history that goes right back to the
beginnings of the sport. The old Pen y Pass
Hotel (now the Youth Hostel) was famous for
the Christmas and Easter climbing parties that
Geoffrey Winthrop Young organised before the
Great War. It was on the nearby cliffs of
Lliwedd that early Everesters like George
Mallory developed their rockclimbing
technique. Since the Second World War the
focus of attention has switched to the Llanberis
Pass (on the far side of Pen y Pass in the
picture) – which is now one of the most
important centres of rockclimbing in Britain.

Hasselblad   150mm   f5.6   1/250   81A   RDP

ACKNOWLEDGEMENTS

This book would not have been possible without the help of a considerable number of people. In particular my thanks go to those who assisted me on some of the more difficult photographic assignments, which involved, among other things, carrying very heavy loads of camping and photographic gear to remote locations: Alan Brown and Phil Sharkey (Garbh Choire), David Granger (Ben Nevis, An Teallach, and Suilven), David Hope (Loch Coruisk), Zbyszek Kotowicz (Eskdale and Scafell Pike), Martin Middleton (Torridon), and Andrew Robson (Strone Ulladale and Applecross). Their cheerful support in difficult conditions was greatly appreciated.

All the climbers featured in the photographs are acknowledged (where known) in the 'Notes to the Plates', but I would like to express particular gratitude to those who helped me obtain specific shots: Matt Andrews, Rosamund Bell, Julie Clover, Marisa Damaso, Johnny Dawes, Neil Drummond, John Edwards, Gareth Evans, Gareth Fletcher, Paul Gabell, Rick Garbutt, Nick Gregory, Simon Hardie, Andy Letchford, Nick McEvett, Stuart Mitchell, Ben Moon, Simon Ogsden, Louise Osborne, Kerry Owen, Mark Pretty, Paul Pritchard, Zak Sargent, John Thedham, Simon Tong, Dave Weale, and Lisa White.

Thanks are also due to the following for their generous hospitality: my aunt, Hazel Fallon (Perth), Iwan Arfon Jones (Llanberis), Ian Nicolson (King's House Hotel), Dave Hanna (Ballachulish), and Brian Fairclough (Stornaway); to Gary Haley for the maps; to Felicity Butler for her invaluable information on adrenalin and related medical matters; to Cotswold Camping for camping and mountaineering equipment; to Promises (London) and Eastern Photocolour (Edinburgh) for the bulk of the photographic processing; to Teamwork (Covent Garden) for their excellent back-up service for the Wista 5 × 4 camera; and to my agent, John Parker, for his very helpful editorial advice.

Finally, I am indebted to my immediate family – Peter and Dorothy, John and Vivien – for their very substantial support throughout.

Plates are shown in **bold** type